Around the
World
in 1776

John Trumbull   *The Declaration of Independence*   YALE UNIVERSITY ART GALLERY

Around the World in 1776

FON W. BOARDMAN, JR.

HENRY Z. WALCK INC./NEW YORK

Copyright © 1975 by Fon W. Boardman, Jr.
ISBN: 0-8098-3124-4
Library of Congress Catalog Card Number: 74-19710
Printed in the United States of America

Library of Congress Cataloging in Publication Data

Boardman, Fon Wyman, date
    Around the world in 1776.

    Bibliography: p.
    Includes index.
    SUMMARY: An overview of what was going on in the world
while the Declaration of Independence was being signed in Philadelphia.
    1. History, Modern—18th century—Juvenile literature. 2. United
States—Politics and government—Revolution, 1775-1783—Juvenile
literature. [1. History, Modern—18th century. 2. United States—History—Revolution, 1775-1783] I. Title.
D288.B62   909.7   74-19710
ISBN 0-8098-3124-4

Contents

Around
the
World
in 1776

1

Philadelphia

July 2, 1776

In England, Robert Adam, architect and designer, was in the process of building a handsome house for the Countess of Home in Portman Square, London.

In France, the Comte de Buffon was hard at work on his *Histoire Naturelle* which he had begun in 1749.

In Germany, Carl Philipp Emanuel Bach was busy as director of music for the five leading churches of Hamburg.

In Spain, Francisco Goya was living in Madrid where he was designing tapestries to be produced by the royal factory.

In Austria, Wenzel Anton Kaunitz had completed almost a quarter of a century of service as a high government official.

In Russia, Ivan Afanasyevich Dmitrevsky held the highest position in the St. Petersburg Theater, both as an actor and as an administrator.

In Africa, hundreds of Black men and women were penned up in the dungeons of west coast "slave castles," awaiting shipment to the New World.

In China, Ch'ien-lung, the fourth emperor of the all-powerful Manchu Dynasty, was in his fortieth year on the throne.

In India, Warren Hastings, first British governor general, was involved in a bitter power struggle with his council.

* * * * *

In Philadelphia, in the British colony of Pennsylvania, a group of men were too busy with their own pressing concerns to give much thought to such events, even if they were aware of them. These men were representatives from all of Great Britain's North American colonies, except Canada, and they had been assembled in Philadelphia for a little more than a year, as the Second Continental Congress. Now, on July 2, 1776, they prepared to vote on a resolution that declared the colonies they represented should no longer be part of, or ruled by, the British Empire.

This small body of men came from thirteen different colonies, stretching from the Canadian border southward through Georgia. On the map the colonies appeared to cling precariously to the eastern edge of an enormous land mass that dwarfed the farms and cities of the colonies with their total population of approximately 2,500,000 people. Philadelphia, with a population of about 40,000, was the largest city in the colonies and larger than most of the cities of England. The members of the Congress found themselves in a bustling, prosperous city of 6,057 dwelling places, 287 business establishments, shops and warehouses, and 7 newspapers. As a leading center of commerce and culture, it was a fitting meeting place for the Continental Congress. A further consideration in those days of slow transportation was its geographical location, almost equally distant from the extreme northern and southern colonies.

Thirteen years before the Congress debated the momentous resolution on independence a decisive turning point had been reached in the relationship of the colonies with the mother country. It was at the end of the Seven Years War (1756–63). Fought in North America, Europe and India, this struggle was truly a worldwide war. Great Britain, Prussia and Hanover on one side were pitted against France, Austria, Russia, Saxony, Sweden and Spain on the other. In North America it was known as the French and Indian War. On the continent of Europe, it was primarily a struggle for supremacy in the Germanic lands, between Austria and Prussia. In the rest of the world, the war was the end result of French and British colonial and trade rivalry.

The war ended with a complete victory for Britain over France. By the Treaty of Paris in 1763, France ceded her overseas possessions, except for a few islands, to England. The latter thus became supreme in India, took over Canada which had hitherto been a French possession, and became the world's leading colonial and sea power.

The defeat of the French meant much to the American colonists. No longer were they in danger of attack from the French and their Indian allies, and so they were not as dependent on the mother country for military assistance. In addition, many of the colonists' families had been in America for several generations and they no longer felt as "English" as they once had. The British government, on the other hand, thought that the colonies, through taxation, should contribute toward the cost of the recent war and to the future defense of the empire, including North America. Britain also imposed economic controls that the colonists believed benefited the mother country at their expense.

The British, whose taxes were higher than those of the Americans, pointed out that most if not all the money raised from any new taxes would be spent in North America. Accordingly, Parliament passed a Stamp Act in 1765 to apply to the colonies. It was the first direct, internal tax imposed on America by Parliament, and the first of any kind except for customs duties. It was, comparatively, a heavy tax and a great nuisance. The tax had to be paid on every kind of legal paper, all licenses, including marriage licenses, even dice and playing cards; and, in the case of newspapers, at the high rate of one shilling for every copy printed.

The reaction of the colonists was immediate and strong. In many places men formed local chapters of an organization known as the Sons of Liberty. The homes and offices of British officials were attacked by such groups who seized and burned the stamped paper. A Stamp Act Congress met in New York City in October, 1765, and adopted a petition to King George III and to Parliament which contended that freeborn Englishmen could not be taxed without their consent. Since the colonies were not represented in Parliament, the Stamp Act, the Congress asserted, meant taxation without representation. The British Parliament backed down in March, 1766, and repealed the Stamp Act, but in doing so it went out of its way to declare that it had the right to impose any laws it chose on the balky colonies.

A little more than a year later, in June, 1767, Parliament passed the Townshend Acts, named for Charles Townshend, the British chancellor of the exchequer. These laws were intended to collect money from the colonies by putting customs duties on imports of glass, lead, paint, paper and tea — the tea being imported through the British East India Company. Many Americans, especially in Massachusetts, began to boycott British goods. Troops were sent from England to enforce the laws and to put down demonstrations. Agitation against the Townshend Acts culminated on March 5, 1770, in Boston, when the Redcoats — who had been constantly tormented and taunted by gangs of men and boys — fired into a riotous crowd. Three men were killed and two died later of wounds. These victims of the Boston Massacre, as the event came to be known, were hailed as patriotic martyrs, and the bad feeling between colonists and the home country was further aggravated.

Once again Parliament gave in—to some extent. The Townshend Acts were repealed in 1770, but the tax on tea was retained, partly to aid the financially hard-pressed East India Company, and partly to affirm once more Parliament's claim that it had a legal right to tax the colonies. Again, the colonists replied by protest and physical demonstrations. They tried to prevent merchants from accepting shipments of tea and were largely successful. A band of Americans disguised as Indians boarded three tea ships in Boston harbor on December 16, 1773, and dumped the tea into the water. This event has been famous ever since as the Boston Tea Party.

The British government responded in 1774 with a new series of acts of Parliament designed to punish the rebellious Americans. These "Intolerable Acts," also known as the "Coercive Acts," closed the port of Boston until the Bostonians paid for the tea thrown into the harbor, restricted the government of the colony, and set up a Quartering Act whereby private homes in any colony could be commandeered to house British troops.

The imposition of the Intolerable Acts resulted in the calling of the First Continental Congress, modeled on the Stamp Act Congress of 1765, which met in Philadelphia from September 5 to October 26, 1774. All the colonies were represented except Georgia. The Congress expressed its grievances against British policy, organized a further boycott of British goods, and decided to meet again on May 10, 1775.

But before any more such meetings were held, the struggle took a further turn toward armed conflict. On April 19, 1775, a British force in Boston, hoping to avoid warfare by seizing the military supplies of the Massachusetts patriots in Lexington and Concord, marched out of the city. Alerted by the famous ride of Paul Revere, the colonials gave battle. They killed or wounded more than two hundred Redcoats, and thus fought the first military engagement of the American Revolution. When the Second Continental Congress did meet, one of its first acts, on June 15, was to appoint George Washington commander-in-chief of a new Continental Army. Two days later the Battle of Bunker Hill, fought in the Boston area, emphasized further that the dispute between the colonies and the government of King George III could be settled only by force of arms.

Although the Congress had no representatives from Canada, its leaders were well aware of that very large but sparsely settled land to the north. The First Congress in 1774 had invited the people of Quebec to send delegates to the Second Congress the following year. The invitation was rejected. The English-speaking people of Canada seemed content with their relations with Great Britain. The French-speaking Canadians, of whom there were about 100,000, stayed neutral. They were well treated by their recent conquerors, and if Canada and the colonies to the south should join forces, they would be a national and linguistic minority group. Canada, in fact, became a haven for those who opposed the Revolution. When the British Army evacuated its forces from Boston in 1776, large numbers of colonial Loyalists, also called Tories, fled to Halifax, Nova Scotia. Later, when the British abandoned New York City in 1783, still more Americans who did not support the Revolution emigrated to Canada.

The Quebec Act, which Americans considered one of the Intolerable Acts of 1774, did much to appease the French-Canadians, as well as to outrage the thirteen colonies. For practical purposes it established the Roman Catholic Church in French Canada, and guaranteed the French system of law. This aroused strong feeling on the part of Protestants in the colonies. At the same time, even stronger protests arose when Great Britain expanded the territory of Quebec to include all the land north of the Ohio River. The Americans saw this as an attempt to block their movement westward from the Atlantic Coast colonies.

In the summer of 1775, while still hoping to persuade Canada to join the revolt, but fearing that if she did not, the British would use Canada as a base for attacking the colonies, the Continental Congress prepared to send a military expedition northward. General Richard Montgomery led one force up the Lake Champlain route and in November captured Montreal. A second force, led by Benedict Arnold in September, headed for Quebec by way of Maine. His force reached its goal in a badly weakened condition from the hardships of the march. Late in the year General Montgomery joined Arnold and on the very last day of 1775 they launched an attack on the city of Quebec. The assault was unsuccessful, Montgomery was killed and Arnold wounded. The Americans continued to besiege the city until spring, but when Hessian mercenary troops arrived to reinforce the British, the Americans were pushed back out of Canada.

The commander of the successful defense of Canada was Sir Guy Carleton (1724–1808), who became governor of Quebec in 1767. He favored the French Canadians and the Quebec Act was his idea as a means of building loyalty to the British crown to offset the rebelliousness of the thirteen colonies. He had previously distinguished himself in the French and Indian War, and on July 6, 1776, he was nominated by his sovereign to be a Knight of the Bath.

Meanwhile, the Second Continental Congress continued its meetings. It now held its sessions in the brick Pennsylvania State House, which later became known as Independence Hall. All thirteen colonies had representatives present, and for the first time Thomas Jefferson of Virginia and Benjamin Franklin of Pennsylvania were delegates. That spring of 1776 marked the first time Jefferson went outside his native Virginia on public business.

Richard Henry Lee, aristocratic delegate from Jefferson's colony, on June 7 offered a resolution to the Congress which said in part that:

> These United Colonies are, and of a right ought to be, free and independent States, that they are absolved from all allegiance to the British Crown, and that all political connection between them and the State of Great Britain is, and ought to be, totally dissolved.

Because some of the delegates had not made up their minds, or had not received instructions from the governments of the colonies they represented, a vote on the resolution was put off until early July.

In anticipation of the coming vote, a committee was appointed on June 11, to draft a fitting and comprehensive statement of the colonies' decision. The committee consisted of Jefferson, Franklin, John Adams of Massachusetts, Roger Sherman of Connecticut and Robert R. Livingston of New York. Jefferson, thirty-three years old and the youngest member of the committee except for Livingston, was given the task of drafting a declaration. His draft was gone over by the committee, especially by Adams and Franklin, and some changes were made before it was submitted to Congress on behalf of the committee on June 28.

Discussion of Lee's resolution was resumed on July 1, and the next day it was adopted, with all the colonies voting for it except New York, which abstained pending authorization from home. Independence, in principle, had now been agreed on. It remained to debate, amend and edit the formal declaration of which Jefferson was the primary author.

Thomas Jefferson (1743–1826) was then a lanky young man with reddish hair. He may not have looked mature enough for the momentous task assigned to him, but he proved he was. He had attended William and Mary College (entering the same year George III became king), had studied law and read widely. Above all, he was an unusually intelligent man. Among the authors he had studied were the English and French philosophers and political theorists, such as John Locke and Voltaire. Following such thinkers, Jefferson believed in reason and inquiry, in searching always for the truth. He further believed that ideas should be put to practical use in politics and in life in general; and that knowledge could help to achieve better government and better relations among people. More specifically, as the Declaration of Independence showed, he believed in natural law and in natural rights that applied to all. Thus the people were sovereign, and one aim of government was to create a better life for all citizens. Out of this basic philosophy came such statements in the Declaration as the world-famous:

> We hold these truths to be self-evident, that all men are created equal, that they are endowed by their Creator with certain unalienable rights, that among these are life, liberty, and the pursuit of happiness. That to secure these rights, governments are instituted among men, deriving their just powers from the consent of the governed.

In thinking and writing from this point of view, Thomas Jefferson was a true believer in the general intellectual attitude of the Enlightenment, or the Age of Reason. The Enlightenment as an overall term sums up the mainstream of thought in eighteenth-century Europe and America. France was the heart of the Enlightenment, with the best-known thinkers and writers and the most vociferous advocates of reform. The intellectual fathers of the Enlightenment, though, were two Englishmen, John Locke (1632–1704) and

Isaac Newton (1642–1727). Newton formulated the law of gravitation and demonstrated to the world that there were certain rules in the physical universe that were steady and unchanging. Locke's thought and writings did for human nature what Newton did for the physical world. Locke wrote convincingly of the natural rights of people, and of the need for government to protect liberty and property and to govern through laws that would benefit the people, not the rulers.

Building on the work of Newton and Locke, the intellectuals of the eighteenth century attempted to find laws in the social sciences and in human and governmental relationships that would be the equivalent of Newton's laws in the physical world. They transferred the scientific spirit of inquiry and investigation to politics and religion. The Enlightenment stood for the rational approach, the secular view of the world rather than the traditional Christian outlook, and the belief that in this way progress toward a better world—even a perfect world—was possible.

In that late eighteenth-century world, no city in America was a more appropriate location for the writing of the Declaration of Independence than Philadelphia. Here, more than in any other of the colonial cities and towns, the ideas of the Enlightenment were welcomed and discussed. No one was a better living example of Enlightenment thinking than Philadelphia's leading citizen, Benjamin Franklin. From the City of Brotherly Love, no longer predominantly Quaker in spirit, the new outlook on life of the Age of Reason was carried to other towns and to rural areas. The story of the framing of the Declaration of Independence in 1776 cannot be told without relating it to the intellectual spirit of the time, any more than it can be considered without relating it to the geographical and political world.

In this setting, the delegates to the Second Continental Congress went about their work. Meanwhile, other events were taking place around the world. The members of the Congress were aware of some of these, unaware of others; concerned and affected by some events, untouched by others. Of most immediate concern to them were the policies and acts of the government of Great Britain.

2

Great Britain
Two Revolutions

Great Britain, with whose government the thirteen colonies were at odds in 1776, was a prosperous, self-satisfied constitutional monarchy. It was ruled by men who, though they may have meant well, were often wrong in what they thought was best for the nation. The island kingdom, besides having the largest navy and the most colonies, was strong financially and was on the verge of leading the world into a new industrial era.

On the continent of Europe, across the British Channel, Spain and Austria were declining in power. France remained a greater military force on land than Britain, but was less powerful otherwise. Prussia and Russia were rapidly rising nations, but they in no way threatened British interests. Dutch naval and mercantile strength had been declining for some time, and the Netherlands no longer could compete with the British in either sphere.

It was a period in which European civilization was

spreading around the world, carrying with it its social customs and styles of dress and religion, as well as its science, technology, and military and economic systems. With this process came European military and political dominance over the whole of the Western Hemisphere and large parts of Africa and Asia. The science, technology, culture and ideals of the European peoples were well on the way toward securing a predominant position all over the globe. Although this development brought some economic and other advantages to almost all Europeans, for the time being it benefited chiefly those already holding power by hereditary means, together with the rising merchant and industrial class.

In Britain there was more democracy than elsewhere, although the nation was far from the "one person, one vote" ideal of later generations. Britons enjoyed more civil liberties and greater freedom of speech than did people on the continent, while in economic affairs men of no rank by birth and no inherited wealth could become rich and powerful by their own efforts and good fortune. Perhaps the greatest difference, though, between England and the large continental nations was that they were ruled by absolute monarchs whereas England had a constitutional monarch, whose powers were quite specifically defined, and who shared political power with an elected parliament.

This Great Britain of 1776 had a population, in England, Wales and Scotland, of about 8,000,000 people, of whom at least 750,000 lived in London, making it the largest city of Europe. In keeping with England's importance in the world, London was a bustling, growing city, much admired by visitors. It was estimated that 43,000 houses were built in the city between 1762 and 1779. Some of these were palatial homes of rich landowners and newly wealthy businessmen, and their construction produced some of London's most attractive squares. A German visitor in this period praised the many streets paved with stone but especially admired the oil lamps which, he said, made London's street lighting "outstanding and incomparable to anything of its kind."

London was the seat of a government that was thought by some to be the best in the world. It was a government made up of an hereditary king; his ministers and advisers (who served as individuals rather than as members of political parties, although there were bound to be groupings of men of like interests); and a parliament of two houses, one elected, one hereditary.

The king was George III (1738–1820), grandson of George II. He belonged to the house of Hanover, which was a Germanic territory and whose ruler in 1692 had been raised to the rank of elector of the Holy Roman Empire. In 1701 the British Parliament passed the Act of Settlement, which provided that if King William III and Princess Anne (later Queen Anne) died without heirs, the throne should go to Sophia, the electress of Hanover, because she was the granddaughter of King James I of England. The succession was to be passed on to her heirs, providing they were Protestants, and so, when Queen Anne died in 1714, George I, elector of Hanover and great-grandfather of George III, became the first British sovereign of the house of Hanover. George III was the first native-born sovereign in almost seventy-five years, and he became king of Great Britain and Ireland in 1760 when he was twenty-two years of age.

Fairly tall, with an open countenance, George was serious and methodical. He was resolved to be a hard-working king, ruling for the benefit of the people as he saw it, but also restoring to the monarchy some of the prestige and power which had been gradually wearing away. He was a great contrast to his grandfather, George II, who had led an irregular private life and who always retained foreign, Germanic ways. The public soon came to like the third

George and to admire his plain, somewhat countrified way of life. George tried to see that his eldest son, who was born two years after he became king, and who later ruled as George IV, had a proper education. In the midst of his troubles with the colonies in 1776, he named new tutors for the boy: the Bishop of Lichfield and Lord Bruce.

In matters such as this, George III certainly was well intentioned but, long after he was dead, an unkind poet wrote of him:

George III
  Ought never to have occurred
One can only wonder
  At so grotesque a blunder.

George summed himself up better when he wrote:

I do not pretend to any superior abilities, but will give place to no one in meaning to preserve the freedom, happiness and glory of my dominions, and all their inhabitants, and to fulfill the duty to my God and my neighbor in the most extended sense. That I have erred is undoubted, otherwise I should not be human, but I flatter myself all unprejudiced persons will be convinced that whenever I have failed it has been from the head not the heart.

With the American colonies, George failed, no matter how well he meant. When trouble first arose, most colonists made a distinction between the king and the British government. They were favorably inclined toward George and wanted to be loyal to their monarch. Their complaint was against the king's ministers. George wanted to conciliate the colonies, but he insisted stubbornly that his policies were for their own good and therefore they should accept them. The colonies disagreed and became just as stubborn in their opposition, and by the summer of 1775, George grew bitter toward the American rebels and declared the colonies to be in open rebellion against the crown. Thus, by the summer of 1776, when the Declaration of Independence was drafted, the Continental Congress in preparing to list in that document the various grievances against Great Britain, asserted that "the history of the present King of Great Britain is a history of repeated injuries and usurpations, all having in direct object the establishment of an absolute tyranny over these States."

Most of the rebels' wrath fell on two of George's ministers who were in high offices in 1776. One was Lord Frederick North (1732–92), who entered Parliament at the age of twenty-two and who was named prime minister in 1770. Lord North was an intelligent man, a loyal supporter of the king, but he misjudged the temper of the colonists, for he did not believe they would continue to defy the British government. His angry reaction to the Boston Tea Party culminated in the Intolerable Acts. When the Revolution began in earnest in 1776, he offered to resign his post, but George could find no one acceptable to replace him. North stayed in office until 1782.

The other chief enemy from the American point of view was Lord George Germain (1716–85), whose career in the army in the Seven Years War ended in his court-martial and dismissal for insubordination during a battle. In spite of his army difficulties, he was appointed secretary of state for the colonies in 1775, and he was zealous in his efforts to defeat the Americans. His military plans, especially the scheme of 1777 to split the colonies apart by the Saratoga campaign in New York, failed, and so Germain must bear a large share of the blame for the British disaster. He, too, resigned in 1782 after news of the final American victory at Yorktown, Virginia.

The colonies had some defenders in Parliament. The elder statesman among them was William Pitt, first Earl of

Chatham (1708–78), who opposed the government's policy toward America. Pitt was not liked by the king, who forced him out of the office of prime minister in 1760, although it was Pitt's policies that were then winning the Seven Years War for Britain. From 1767 on Pitt suffered from a mental illness and was able to take but little part in public life. He was so ill in 1776 that he was unable to attend Parliament at all, but his position was well known. He wanted to conciliate the colonies and was willing to concede them anything except outright independence.

The Marquess of Rockingham (1730–82) had earlier been prime minister for a year, and in 1766 had put through Parliament the repeal of the Stamp Act. He continued to support attempts to keep peace with the colonies, and in 1775 he backed a proposal to withdraw the British troops from Boston. Rockingham recorded a further protest in October, 1776, when he moved in Parliament to put an end to the fighting in the colonies and let them go their own way, but his motion failed.

The most intellectual friend of America and the most effective speaker in Parliament on that side was Edmund Burke (1729–97). Burke was first elected to Parliament in 1765 and served until 1794, almost all that time being in opposition to the king's ministers. He acted as agent for the colony of New York, and corresponded with the legislature there to advise members on proposed visits to England. His two most famous speeches on the American problem were delivered in Parliament in 1774 and 1775. The former dealt with taxation while the latter pleaded eloquently for conciliation. He seconded a motion in Parliament in November, 1776, that called for revision of all the laws that were disturbing the colonies. The motion failed and Burke and his friends gave up hope of ending the conflict.

Although in general agreement with Burke as to the rights of the colonies, no man was further from him in other ways than John Wilkes (1727–97). His personal life was often dissolute and he was a member of the infamous Hell-Fire Club whose activities were notorious for their low moral tone. In politics, however, Wilkes was an honest man, even if demagogic in his manners, and he became the idol of the common people of London. Wilkes was arrested and jailed for writing critically of a speech from the throne. He was then elected to Parliament several times but was refused his seat, although he was legally entitled to it, chiefly because the majority of the members detested him. He was finally allowed to take his seat in 1774, and that same year he was elected lord mayor of London. Wilkes opposed the government on its American policy, and in 1776 he tried to reform Parliament so that its membership would better reflect the population as a whole. In the course of defending his proposal he used words not unlike Jefferson's:

> We ought always to remember this important truth, acknowledged by every free state, that all government is instituted for the good of the mass of the people to be governed; that they are the original fountain of power. . . .

Wilkes was much admired in America and exchanged letters with some of the patriot leaders in Boston. Jefferson and others like him looked to Wilkes and his followers to reform the government of Great Britain so that it would not be at odds with America. Jefferson, in fact, obtained copies of his speeches for his library, but in the end Wilkes was a disappointment to men such as Jefferson because his personality and methods made so many enemies in high places that he could accomplish little.

The British government had problems with Ireland as well as with America. Ireland had its own parliament, but was completely subject to Great Britain. Anglo-Irish families who had taken up residence and large landholdings in

Ireland in the seventeenth century dominated the country. Many of them were now absentee landlords who cared little for the welfare of the Irish. The government in London sent out the higher officials to rule the island, Lord Buckinghamshire being appointed viceroy in 1776. The year before, the British had put an embargo on all Irish goods going to the American colonies as a punishment for the latter. The result was severe hardship and distress in Ireland.

The prevailing political and economic theory of "mercantilism," as practiced by Great Britain, was another source of the trouble with the colonies. Under a mercantilist policy, the government of a country exercised full control over foreign trade and shipping. Every nation tried to sell as much as possible to other nations, and to buy as little as possible from them. The goal was to accumulate large amounts of gold and other precious metals. The theory held that this made a nation strong in relation to others with which it might go to war.

To make such a policy effective, a nation with colonies restricted all trade with them to goods carried in its own ships. Furthermore, the colonies were supposed to devote their energies to supplying raw materials to the mother country, and they were to buy all their manufactured goods from the homeland. Thus, from the mercantilist point of view, the laws that the colonists saw as restricting their natural development would, overall, benefit both the colonies and the mother country. Both would prosper by playing their assigned parts while keeping all other countries out in the cold. By 1776 this conflict of interest had come to a head since the Americans wanted to manufacture some of their own goods, and to trade freely with other countries, especially the West Indies.

Seeds of the destruction of this mercantilist system lay not only in the revolt of the colonies, but also in scientific and technical developments taking place in the very heart of the empire, the British Isles. The most basic of all industries, agriculture, was changing rather rapidly. To meet the needs of a growing population, new devices and new methods were tried to increase the food supply. Prizes were offered, agricultural societies were founded and, in 1776, there appeared the first issue of the *Farmers' Magazine*. Also at this time, more and more of the land of England was being "enclosed." This process ended the pattern of many small landholdings cultivated by a number of farmers, in favor of larger groupings that allowed more efficient use of the arable land. Small landholders were squeezed out by the rich and powerful estate owners, and land held in common by all the people of a village disappeared. The result was hardship for some, but food production was increased and costs were lowered.

The Industrial Revolution, which in less than one hundred years transformed a great deal of the world, started in England in the mid-eighteenth century and was, in the long run, as important as the American Revolution. If one chooses any particular year for its start, 1760—the year in which George III ascended the British throne—is as good a choice as any. The two revolutions thus were moving along the same time track, and were not without effect on each other.

It was no accident that Great Britain, though much of its energy was taken up with winning, holding and losing an empire, was the birthplace of the Industrial Revolution. As oppressive as the government seemed to the members of the Continental Congress debating in Philadelphia, the fact remained that Great Britain provided a freer atmosphere for business, industrial and financial initiative than any other country. Its recent triumph in the Seven Years War had put it in the position of having the capital funds needed to invest in business enterprise. A growing population provided workers for factories and consumers for the goods they produced. Of considerable importance, too, was the developing transportation system, especially the building of canals, in which England pioneered. By 1776 many miles of canals spread like a web over inland England, and others were under construction.

In the technological field, newly invented machines made it possible to produce more goods, faster and more cheaply, in factories employing large numbers of people. This accelerated the change from rural to urban life, the growth of large cities with slums, and the garnering of great wealth by a comparatively small number of men who were capable and tough enough to come out on top in a highly competitive situation.

The inventors and innovators at the heart of this change included men such as James Watt (1736–1819) and Josiah Wedgwood (1730–95). Watt developed the steam engine into the kind of machinery needed in the latter part of the eighteenth century to accelerate the growth of the Industrial Revolution. Other people had already contributed to the harnessing of steam. In about 1711 Thomas Newcomen (1663–1729) devised an engine that successfully pumped water. Watt first began to try to improve the steam engine after 1757, while he was "Mathematical Instrument Maker to the University" in Glasgow, Scotland. Out of his experiments came the first steam engine used for some process more complicated than pumping water. Watt greatly improved the efficiency of such engines by devising a separate condenser for the steam, apart from the cylinder itself. By this innovation and others, he produced a machine that could be used for many purposes, including blast-furnace operations involved in iron smelting, a basic factor in the new industrialism. Watt patented his engine in 1769, but it was 1776 before two of them were actually put to work.

Wedgwood, who was the thirteenth and youngest child in his family, started in business for himself when he was twenty-one, and between then and his death became the greatest pottery manufacturer in the world. He built the new village of Etruria, which included homes for his workmen as well as factories. Eventually, he employed 20,000 people. He was an outstanding example of the successful man of the Industrial Revolution, planning new and more attractive products, organizing their production efficiently, and finding methods for distributing and selling them all over the world. In 1774 he completed a dinner service for Catherine the Great of Russia. The set consisted of 952 pieces of cream-colored ware.

A book that was as influential as the Declaration of Independence was published in England in March, 1776. It was *The Wealth of Nations,* by Adam Smith (1723–90). In his book the Scottish economist and professor of moral philosophy expounded the benefits of the division of labor, argued that it was the labor expended that gave value to the goods produced, and presented the popular doctrine that came to be called "laissez-faire." Smith believed that if every man labored in his own economic self-interest, the overall result would be in the public interest. He opposed all restrictions on manufacturing and trade, although he agreed that at times a nation must control its trade in the interest of national security. Smith, who was a friend of David Hume, the philosopher, and who had met Voltaire, leader of the French Enlightenment, wanted the American colonies represented in Parliament. In his book he wrote of the colonies: "They will be one of the foremost nations of the world."

Late eighteenth-century England could boast a far better record in the realm of literature and journalism than in government. Except for France, no other nation at this time produced so many writers who have been accorded permanent high rank. The development of printing technology, and the consequent publication of more papers and journals, helped spread the ideas of the age. For the first time, a person could make a living as a writer and need not depend on a patron.

Samuel Johnson (1709−84), son of a poor bookseller, was England's leading literary figure. He had been writing for about forty years, and in fact most of his major works were written before 1776. His writings included poetry, plays and many biographical studies. For two years, beginning in 1750, he issued a twice-weekly periodical, *The Rambler*, which he wrote almost entirely by himself. His famous dictionary of the English language was published in 1755. He became, and remained, a virtual dictator of literary taste−as much by his wit and great talent as a conversationalist, as by his writings. His wit was sometimes savage, but under his gruff exterior he was a kindly man. Johnson was one of the two founders of the Literary Club, first known simply as the Club, in 1764. Representing the peak of the intellectual world, the club met every week at the Turk's Head Tavern in the Soho section of London.

Johnson had little sympathy with the colonies. In *Taxation no Tyranny*, which he published the year before the Declaration of Independence, he wrote of America: "How is it that we hear the loudest yelps for liberty among the drivers of Negroes?" In fact, Johnson seemed to have an intense dislike of America and Americans. At one time he remarked: "Sir, they are a race of convicts, and ought to be content with anything we allow them short of hanging," and on another occasion, during the Revolution, he asserted: "I am willing to love all mankind, except an American."

In 1775, Johnson wrote his account of a tour of the Hebrides, which he had taken in 1773 with his friend, James Boswell (1740−95). Without Boswell, who later produced a famous biography of his friend, Johnson would be far less well-known today. Boswell, a Scotsman, first met Johnson in 1763, and from then on spent much time with him, traveling and noting down Johnson's comments on many matters.

The great man expressed himself both well and freely —
and sometimes savagely when he disliked a person or an
idea. Boswell made a career of meeting famous people, such
as Wilkes in England and, in France, Voltaire and Rousseau.

Boswell also met and questioned the great philosopher
and historian, David Hume. Hume, who was born in Scotland in 1711, had long since written his most important
works, especially those in which he sought to complete and
correct John Locke's thinking in terms of his own view of
the world. Now he was dying, but on July 7, 1776, Boswell
visited him in Edinburgh and discussed with him his views
on religion and immortality. Hume died on August 25.

A dozen years earlier, while in Rome, Edward Gibbon
(1737–94) had conceived the idea for a definitive history of
The Decline and Fall of the Roman Empire, but the first of six
volumes did not appear until early 1776. The history was
immediately popular and sold very well. Gibbon, a member
of the Literary Club, was under five feet tall and very fat.
He overdressed and was affected in manner, so that he was
much ridiculed in spite of his literary success. A member of
Parliament from 1774 to 1783, he supported Lord North and
was a violent opponent of the American Revolution.

The Burneys, father and daughter, were also prominent in
the literary world. Frances (Fanny) Burney (1752–1840) was
at work on her first novel in 1776. It was published successfully but anonymously in 1778 as *Evelina.* Fanny became
a friend of Johnson and his circle, but women were not
allowed membership in the Literary Club itself. Charles
Burney (1726–1814) was a musician as well as a historian of
the subject. The first volume of his *History of Music* appeared in 1776 and was very well received. That same year
John Hawkins (1719–89), an attorney and justice of the
peace, also brought out a history of music. In five volumes,
it was a storehouse of information, but suffered from the
competition with Dr. Burney's book.

In the world of European art, the latter part of the eighteenth century was marked by the aesthetic movement called neo-classicism. This was in part a reaction to the over-elaborateness of the baroque and rococo styles. Baroque art was the predominant style of the seventeenth century. While it sought balance and wholeness, it was also art on a large scale, with much energy and movement. Size and impressiveness were important factors, especially in baroque architecture. The rococo style, which emerged in France around 1700, was used primarily for decoration and ornamentation. It was fanciful and in the opinion of some, it was ornate, excessive and meaningless. Neo-classicism, as its name implies, reflected a renewed interest in antiquities, and in the classical Greek and Roman eras. Thus neo-classical art, in contrast with baroque and rococo, copied the simplicity, balance and elegance of Greek and Roman art and architecture.

The leading artists of Great Britain, while naturally influenced by general movements, were primarily portrait painters if for no other reason than that was what people in a position to patronize artists most wanted. Sir Joshua Reynolds (1723–92) was the most important English artist of his day, and perhaps the most significant in all of English art. He was strongly influenced by the neo-classical movement and painted in the "grand manner" — large canvases on which the figures were heroic and aristocratic, exemplifying a type, not an individual. Reynolds achieved enormous success early and painted great numbers of portraits. He was the first president of the Royal Academy of Arts, which was founded in 1768 under the patronage of George III, and he still held the position in 1776. With Dr. Johnson, he was the co-founder of the Literary Club.

Close behind Reynolds in popularity and talent were Thomas Gainsborough (1727–88) and George Romney (1734–1802). Gainsborough, who settled in London in 1774, was an excellent landscape painter who liked to paint rural scenes with rather idealized peasants. However, his portraits were more in demand and he produced many of elegant women. In 1776 he may have been at work on a portrait of the Hon. Mrs. Thomas Graham, a beautiful and charming woman who was the daughter of the British ambassador to Russia, as the painting was started in 1775 and not completed until 1777. His painting of a Mrs. Methuen, another fashionable beauty, was probably one of his works of 1776. Gainsborough did three portraits of George III.

Romney painted many pictures of women and children, such as "The Gower Children" in 1776, which showed neoclassical influence. Romney went to the Drury Lane Theater in London on June 10, 1776, to see the actor David Garrick make his last appearance on the stage and study him with a view to painting him. Richard Wilson (1714–82) was a fine landscape painter but he realized that in order to secure popular acceptance, he had to make his work look as though it were set in Italy, or put in some classical legend. He was one of the founders of the Royal Academy and in 1776 he became its librarian.

Theater-going was popular in London and stage productions were becoming common around the country. It was not a good period for tragedy, but comedy thrived. In general, the theater was reacting from the excess of sentimentality in stage presentations earlier in the century. At this time, one of the most skilled actors of any era was active in the English theater. David Garrick (1717–79), who as a schoolboy studied under Dr. Johnson, became a successful actor, a brilliant dramatist and a theater manager. He instituted some basic changes, such as concealing the stage lighting from the audience and keeping spectators from sitting on the stage. Garrick was manager of the Drury Lane Theater in London from 1747 until 1776. He made his final appearance that spring in a play titled *The Wonder, a Woman never Vexed.*

Garrick gave Sarah Kemble Siddons (1755–1831) her first big opportunity on the London stage. Mrs. Siddons, child of the most distinguished family of British actors, the Kembles, had theatrical experience with her father's traveling company while still very young. When she was brought to Garrick's attention he tried her at the Drury Lane in the 1775–76 season but, surprisingly, she failed. Later she became highly successful and has been called the greatest tragic actress of the English stage.

Upon Garrick's retirement, his share of the Drury Lane Theater was bought by Richard Brinsley Sheridan (1751–1816), one of whose witty comedies of manners, *The Rivals,* had its first performance the previous year. His other permanent addition to the stage, *The School for Scandal,* had its premiere in 1777.

In the field of architecture, furnishings and decoration, as in fine arts, the neo-classical style became predominant. Robert Adam (1728–92) was the most popular practitioner of the time and left his mark on various parts of London. He designed both public and private buildings, and is said to have originated, with his brothers, the idea of constructing a number of private houses together so that the total effect was of one imposing classical structure, as in Portland Place, London. He supervised the details of his buildings down to the last pieces of furniture, and his elegant, graceful and sophisticated style was popular and widely imitated. From 1762 to 1768 Adam was official architect to George III.

Adam's chief rival was Sir William Chambers (1723–96), who was also a busy architect. He was tutor in architecture to King George when he was Prince of Wales, and became a member of the Royal Academy when it was founded in 1768. Chambers began work in 1776 on his masterpiece,

Somerset House, an enormous building on the banks of the Thames River, built to house government offices.

The names of Chippendale, Sheraton and Hepplewhite are still familiar today, and their furniture commands large sums when put on the market. They were equally popular in the eighteenth century when they were designing and producing their wares. The name of Thomas Chippendale (1718–79) is associated most of all with a variety of chairs which he designed. Some were geometrical, some were elaborately carved, and at times his work reflected the Chinese and rococo styles and even the Gothic manner of Europe's Middle Ages. His work was widely copied in America. Thomas Sheraton (1751–1806), a preacher and author of religious books, influenced design mostly through his manuals. These were written later, and he was not yet well known in 1776. He emphasized straight lines and, in general, his graceful designs followed the classical style. Finally, George Hepplewhite (d. 1786), whose furniture designs featured curved, decorative and slender legs, followed much the same style as Adam and his brothers.

Landscape gardening, important when royalty and others can afford large estates, flourished in eighteenth-century England. At this time fashion was abandoning the formal, geometric style in favor of a more natural look — even though artificial means sometimes had to be used to achieve the "natural." The leading practitioner was Lancelot Brown (1715–83), known as "Capability" Brown because he would usually render the opinion, after looking over a prospective area, that it was "capable" of being improved. Brown began life as a kitchen gardener for an English lord. One of his major projects was redesigning the artificial lake on the grounds of Blenheim Palace. The palace, in Oxfordshire, had been constructed in the first quarter of the century. The enormous building was a gift to the first Duke of Marlborough, from Queen Anne, for his military victories.

However talented and successful the leading figures in the arts might have been, science was the sector of intellectual life that grew and changed the most in Western civilization in the eighteenth century. Where the previous century had been one of basic discoveries, such as Newton's findings, the eighteenth was a period in which people built on earlier fundamentals and found practical uses for the new science — as in steam engines, machine tools and other machinery for factories, in weapons of war, in medicine and in aids to navigation. Science became so popular that it was fashionable for upper-class people to perform scientific experiments. In Great Britain, Joseph Priestley (1733–1804) was a combination of clergyman and scientist. He was minister of several Presbyterian churches before turning his chief attention to science in a laboratory in his home. Here in 1774 he isolated oxygen which he called "dephogisticated" air. He also isolated ammonia, chlorine and other gases. He continued his experiments until 1791 when his home and laboratory were wrecked by a mob intent on punishing him for his expressed sympathy for the French Revolution. Three years later Priestley emigrated to the United States and settled in Pennsylvania.

The science of archeology got its start in a somewhat amateurish way. Silbury Hill in Wiltshire, England, is the largest prehistoric artificial mound in all of Europe, and it had long excited the curiosity of many people. It is 130 feet high, and at its base covers five acres of ground. According to tradition, a King Zel was buried in it, along with a solid gold statue of him on horseback. In 1776 the Duke of Northumberland decided to do something to dispel the mystery. He hired some tin miners from Cornwall who dug an eight-foot-square shaft from the top of the mound to ground level, but nothing of interest was found.

The rapidly changing world of the late eighteenth century — the economic and military operations on all continents, the advance of science, the accelerating Industrial Revolution, and the ideas of the Enlightenment—presented organized Christianity with new challenges. Many people felt the need of something different to help them live in a more complex and urban world. In Great Britain, the Church of England did little to face these changing conditions. As a result, some religious leaders set out on their own to preach a more personal religious faith. Among these were the Wesley brothers, John (1703–91) and Charles (1707–88), who became the founders of Methodism, so-called because its adherents were so methodical in their religious studies. Both brothers were well along in years by 1776, and had been to America about forty years before. Now an old foundry at Moorsfield was the center of Methodist work in London. John had preached over 40,000 sermons in the course of his career and Charles had written innumerable hymns.

England has been noted for producing eccentrics, most of them harmless and some later proving to have been not eccentrics but simply ahead of their time. Such a man was Jonas Hanway (1712–86). A man of means, he spent a great deal of time traveling and was also a philanthropist. He agitated for better highways in London and he devised a scheme to keep up the supply of seamen for the navy. His claim to remembrance as a part of the eighteenth-century scene, however, lies in the fact that he is said to have been the first man who made it a habit to carry an umbrella through the streets of London. He had seen them in foreign lands, thought they were a good idea, and carried his umbrella with him for thirty years. At first he was jeered, but eventually his practice was widely adopted.

This was Great Britain in 1776. A world power, a power that was soon to be even greater because of the headstart it had on other nations as the home of the Industrial Revolution. A prosperous, well-meaning country that was having baffling trouble with its American colonies even though they were populated mostly by descendants of immigrants from the British Isles. But while members of the Second Continental Congress were concerned mainly with Great Britain, events were taking place on the continent of Europe which were also to affect the colonies.

3

France

Despotism and
Enlightenment

        France in 1776 was no longer the proudly dominant power it once had been on the continent of Europe. But France still reflected the glamour of a splendid court, and was recognized as the home of the great men of the Enlightenment. France, in fact, was the home of one of the most backward monarchies and some of the most advanced thinkers.

In population, France was the largest nation in Europe, larger even than the Russia of the day, with about 25,000,000 inhabitants. Paris, however, was smaller than London by 100,000 or so persons. France's comparatively large population had been no small factor in its position among its neighbors. While France was a leading manufacturing and commercial nation, it was not yet experiencing, as England was, the drastic changes of the oncoming Industrial Revolution. The guilds, with their stringent regulation of crafts and trades, which prevented change and progress, were strong in France while they were declining in England. This was in part because the influence of mercantilistic thought was stronger in France than in England. French agricultural production was large, most of it the output of thousands of small, peasant-owned farms. France boasted the best road system of the time, with about 25,000 miles of highways under the control of the central government. Half of this was being rebuilt or improved, largely by the labor of peasants who were required to work without pay several days a year on the highways.

Although France was the home of the Enlightenment, and although other governments experimented with the ideas of the Age of Reason, the French government remained mostly in the hands of a monarchy which was becoming less competent and of a parasitical noble class. The gulf between upper and lower classes grew wider.

A new king came to the throne in May, 1774: Louis XVI (1754–93). He was the grandson of Louis XV, and succeeded to the throne because his own father had died of tuberculosis in 1765. Louis XVI was not quite twenty years old, and did not look or act like a monarch. He was not very intelligent, and had received no training from his grandfather in the art of governing a nation where so much depended on the whim of the king. Louis was so obsessed about hunting that when, on a given day, he was unable to indulge in the sport, he wrote simply *rien*, nothing, in his diary, no matter what events were going on in the world around him. His wife, Marie Antoinette (1755–93), daughter of the Austrian Empress Maria Theresa, was no help to him. She was a stronger character, but frivolous, so that her influence on Louis was worse than useless.

Even so, Louis's intentions were good. He made an effort at first to reform his government and he appointed some capable ministers. The foremost of these was Anne Robert Jacques Turgot (1727–81), who was named controller general of finance in 1774. A man of the Enlightenment himself, he took steps to reform the antiquated governmental system. In the course of two years' work, he proposed the abolition of the guilds, reforms in taxation on land that would affect noble landholders, other fiscal economies, free trade in grain and the toleration of Protestants. Members of the privileged classes, including the queen herself, fought Turgot's reforms so strenuously that he was dismissed from office in May, 1776. Two years later Turgot wrote that the Americans were "the *hope* of the world. They may become a *model* to it. They *may* prove by fact that men can be free and yet tranquil."

Among those who brought about Turgot's downfall was the Comte de Maurepas (1701–81) who earlier had selected him for high office. Maurepas became minister of state when only fourteen because, under the system of the time, he had the right to succeed his father. The post was administered for him while he was a minor. Maurepas later supported the French alliance with the American colonies.

Turgot was succeeded by Jacques Necker (1732–1804), a successful banker and a director of the French East India Company. Necker had criticized Turgot and had opposed his economic policies. His wife, Suzanne (1739–94), was as well known as her husband. A writer prominent in literary circles, she was famous for her brilliant salon. About 1776 she founded a hospital which still exists.

While the government of the old regime was struggling less and less successfully to run the country properly, the anti-establishment forces, the thinkers and writers of the Enlightenment, were busier than ever. The French monarchy stood for the divine right of kings, the privileges of unproductive members of the noble class, and the authority of an official and rigid church and clergy. Opposed to all this were those who, in the words of one of them, wanted to "change the general way of thinking," by spreading their ideas as widely as possible.

These men were the *philosophes.* The word didn't quite mean philosopher; rather it meant thinker. They were the political scientists, sociologists, propagandists, editorialists and general intellectual gadflies of the time. They faced censorship and oppression, but they believed they could change the world by enlightening the people. They proposed to do this with their pens and their tongues, without any official organization. In fact, they didn't always agree among themselves.

Surprisingly, from today's point of view, they did not agitate for democracy. They accepted monarchy, even absolute monarchy. Their theory was that the best government would be that headed by an "enlightened despot" who thoroughly believed in the ideas of the Enlightenment, and who would impose them on the people for their good. The *philosophes* stood ready to act as advisers to such rulers, and in several instances they did so.

The *philosophes* made a frontal assault on the organized religious institutions of the day. Most of them accepted the idea of a God who had set the universe going and established laws to govern it. These were the laws discovered by the new science, which they also endorsed. They could not accept a God who interfered with his own laws and they believed, therefore, that formal, organized religion was superfluous and that claims of supernatural revelation must be false. Those who believed in this way were called deists and numbered in their ranks such men as Jefferson and Franklin.

One man symbolized the *philosophes* and the Enlightenment far better than anyone else. He was Voltaire (1694–1778), whose real name was Francois Marie Arouet, and who by 1776 was an old man with only two years to live. He had been in the forefront of the battle of ideas for more than half a century, having written his first successful play when he was only twenty-two. Son of a middle-class lawyer, Voltaire became rich through shrewd investments. His opposition to the old regime and his witty but sharp tongue got him in trouble early. It was partly to escape prosecution that he spent three years in England beginning in 1726. Here he came under the influence of Newton's and Locke's thought. Back in France he became an enemy of the established order, writing plays, fiction, history and denunciations of everything he thought wrong and stupid. While always on the verge of serious trouble with the authorities, he ruled as emperor of the French intellectual world.

Voltaire spent about three years, beginning in 1750, at the court of Frederick II of Prussia, one of the enlightened despots. He had already been elected, in 1746, to the French Academy — the official and most prestigious intellectual body in the nation, which allowed only forty members at a time — but only after having been turned down once. He especially condemned the established church (he was, of course, a deist), defended freedom of speech and, all in all, exhibited every one of the virtues and faults of the men of the Enlightenment. That is, he was powerful on attack, and with his pen he could demolish hypocrisy and stupidity among the enemy. He was not too practical, however, in providing substitutes for the institutions he would destroy. Voltaire was widely read in America, both in French and in translation.

Among Voltaire's many idiosyncrasies was a dislike of William Shakespeare. A new translation of the English playwright in 1776 brought from Voltaire a book denouncing Shakespeare for lack of taste and for being ignorant of the classical rules of drama.

The monument to the *philosophes,* which they erected themselves, was the *Encyclopédie,* which contained articles on the usual important subjects, such as religion, political science, philosophy, education and science. All were written from the point of view of the Age of Reason and directly or indirectly criticized the established outlook of the state and church. The first volume was published in 1751, and the original set was completed by 1772. Supplementary volumes were issued between then and 1780. The editors of the *Encyclopédie* battled almost constantly with critics and censors, and from time to time had to suspend publication. The project cost a large sum for the time—about a million francs—but turned out to be profitable, so great was the interest in this new approach to knowledge. Voltaire, Turgot and Rousseau were among the contributors.

Denis Diderot (1713–84) was the chief editor of the *Encyclopédie* and another of the intellectual giants of the Enlightenment. An affable, gregarious man, he was art critic, literary critic, dramatist and novelist as well as encyclopedia editor. At the invitation of another of the enlightened despots, Catherine the Great of Russia, Diderot spent the years 1773–74 at her court. Diderot was in touch with events in other lands, especially when they related to the *philosophes'* campaign for more freedom. Thus it was that in 1776 he wrote to John Wilkes in England: "I have read with great satisfaction the various orations you have delivered on the affairs of the provincials," (that is, the Americans).

Diderot's co-editor was Jean le Rond d'Alembert (1717–83), who was a mathematician as well as a critic and philosopher. Alembert withdrew as an editor of the *Encyclopédie* in 1758 because of the attacks by the clergy and government officials on his unorthodox views. In 1776 he was serving as secretary of the French Academy, having been named to that post in 1772 after his election to membership in 1754. Another encyclopedist was the Baron d'Holbach (1723–89), who was born in Germany but spent most of his life in France. He was a professed atheist and the most outspoken opponent of Christianity. The encyclopedists owed much to Chrétien Malesherbes (1721–94) who, as the government official with power over book publishing from 1750 to 1763, allowed the work to be published. He believed in freedom of the press and was sympathetic to the *philosophes'* views. He was also a friend and supporter of Turgot and resigned from public office in 1776 when his friend was dismissed.

On the side of the *philosophes* but not totally one of them was Jean Jacques Rousseau (1712–78). He was a man of passion rather than thought. Born in Geneva, Switzerland, Rousseau wandered around Europe as a young man and in 1741 ended up in Paris where he was taken into Diderot's circle. He was given to imagining slights, and managed at one time or another to quarrel with all his friends and fellow intellectuals. Eventually he developed a true persecution mania. Rousseau did not share the current faith in logic and reason and sought his theories of man and society in nature. He saw the American Indians and the African Blacks as "noble savages." He believed that man is naturally good but is corrupted by society. Even so, men leave this natural state and freely join together in an organized society in which they give up their natural liberty to receive certain other benefits. Organized society then depends on mutual agreements and people have a right to change their form of government at will. Jefferson used this basic idea when he contended that in any government the consent of the governed is necessary.

Rousseau's important work had been done before 1776 — such writings as the *Social Contract, Emile,* and his *Confessions.* He was at work in 1776 on *Daydreams of a Solitary Stroller,* which was not published until after he died.

Quite a different kind of person was the Marquis de Sade (1740–1814), who as a young man fought in the Seven Years War. Later, his scandalous conduct resulted in his being imprisoned for brutal and sexual crimes, and he spent most of his life in prison. Here he wrote a number of books which dealt far more openly with sex and sexual practices than was then accepted, and were therefore considered immoral and licentious. Sade was in Italy in 1776, having fled there in 1775 after escaping from prison.

About the same time that Louis XVI ascended the throne, the supremacy of the rococo style in art was coming to an end and, as in other lands, the neo-classical style became the most favored. The older generation of painters, men such as Jean Baptiste Chardin (1699–1779) and Jean Baptiste Greuze (1725–1805), were little affected. Chardin painted simple things, such as still lifes and interiors. The textures and rich colors he gave his still-life subjects, according to some critics, were not equaled by a French painter until Cézanne appeared a century later. Greuze was a pioneer in genre painting—scenes that were anecdotal and extolled rustic virtues. They bore such titles as "The Village Bride" and "The Father's Curse." Diderot said his work was "morality in paint," but the swing to the neo-classical style put him out of fashion.

Of all the painters of the period, Jean Honoré Fragonard (1732–1806) best matched the frivolous, sensuous, and unrealistic temper of the French royal court. His scenes of love and gallantry, such as "Love's Vow," "The Swing" and "Blindman's Buff" are charming technical masterpieces, but the subject matter shows the "beautiful people" of the day living in a lazy, idyllic dream world. "A Young Girl Reading," which was painted about 1776, depicts a pretty, well-dressed young woman who is delightful to look at but who seems to have little relation to the real world.

The pioneer of the neo-classical style was the Comte Joseph-Marie Vien (1716–1809), whose subject matter was chiefly historical. Even he sentimentalized classical anecdotes and allegories. He was named director of the French Academy in Rome in 1776. Vien was the teacher of Jacques-

Louis David (1748–1825), who later, under the Emperor Napoleon, became a virtual dictator in the artistic field. By 1776 David had already won the Prix de Rome for a painting with a classical subject and was in Rome with Vien.

Etienne Maurice Falconet (1716–91) and Jean-Antoine Houdon (1741–1828) were sculptors who preserved the likenesses of leading personalities of the Enlightenment and the American Revolution. Falconet was in Russia in 1776 where he had gone nine years earlier under the patronage of the empress, Catherine the Great. Here he produced a magnificent equestrian statue of Czar Peter the Great. Houdon, in the style of classical mythology, sculpted likenesses of Diderot, Franklin and Washington, among others.

The French theater, with men such as Voltaire interested, prospered. Its leading dramatist was Pierre Augustin Caron de Beaumarchais (1732–99). His first successful play, *Le Barbier de Seville,* on which Rossini later based his opera, was produced in 1775. At this same time Beaumarchais was used by the monarchy as a secret agent, and in the course of his duties became involved in dealings with some American colonial agents. His dummy business concern, Hortalès & Cie, sold arms to the American revolutionaries in 1776–77. The arms were supposed to be paid for with tobacco and other colonial products, but payment was never received in his lifetime.

A successful tragedy, *Mustapha et Zéangir,* by Sebastien Chamfort (1740–94) was produced in 1776. In recognition of this, and for his wit and his other writings, Chamfort was granted a pension by the royal family. Henri Louis Lekain (1729–78) was France's most popular tragic actor and was compared to Garrick. He was first noticed by Voltaire and soon became a star even though he was short, homely and had a harsh voice. He introduced some reforms into the French theater, such as authentic historical costumes and more realistic acting. He was invited to the court of Frederick the Great, as was Voltaire.

The French *philosophes* shared the Age of Reason's fascination with science and the scientific method, and were outstanding in the field of mathematics. In general, the scientists of the time looked upon mathematics as a tool for solving problems in other fields, rather than as a discipline to be pursued for its own sake.

The Marquis de Condorcet (1743–94) was not only a mathematician but also a philosopher and, later, a political leader during the French Revolution. In the temper of the time, he believed that the scientific method he used in mathematics could be applied to everything and would help achieve a perfect society. In 1776 Condorcet issued his edition of the *Pensées* of Blaise Pascal, a seventeenth-century scientist and philosopher. The Marquis de Laplace (1749–1827), although his chief written work did not appear until 1796, established his reputation as a mathematical genius even before 1776. When only eighteen he proved his ability and was made professor of mathematics at the Paris Military School. Laplace used mathematics chiefly in the field of astronomy where he became the most notable theoretical astronomer since Newton.

The founder of modern chemistry was Antoine Laurent Lavoisier (1743–94), who was one of the first to use quantitative methods. Between 1772 and 1777, at about the same time Priestley was at work in England, Lavoisier showed what air consists of, isolated oxygen and gave it its name. Turgot appointed Lavoisier director of a gunpowder commission in 1775, and over the next ten years he reformed the manufacture and supply of gunpowder for France's armed forces.

The Comte de Buffon (1707–88) pioneered in making the study of nature more scientific. Although some of his ideas on the beginnings and the age of the earth outraged theologians and the devout, and some of his theories were later disproved, Buffon's studies and writings laid the foundation for advances in natural science in the nineteenth century. Buffon was keeper of the king's garden in 1776, a position to which he had been appointed in 1739 and which he held to the end of his life. The garden had been founded in 1625 at the king's expense, for the study of medicinal herbs. Buffon used it as a center of research in natural history. He was also at the never-ending task of writing his *Histoire Naturelle* which eventually came to forty-four volumes (the last eight not by Buffon). Publication was spread over more than half a century, from 1749 to 1804. Around the time the American Revolution started, he was engrossed in the nine volumes on birds (1770–83), and the seven on geology (1774–89).

Two men whose names were to be intimately connected with the rebellion of the colonies were on opposite sides of the ocean in 1776 but were soon to change places. Benjamin Franklin, involved in helping to write the Declaration of Independence in June, went to France late in 1776 with two companions to try to secure aid from France. In France, the nineteen-year-old Marquis de Lafayette (1757–1834), who was an officer in the French army, was already enthusiastic about the cause of the colonists and eager to join them. This he did the following year, traveling to Philadelphia where he was at once made a major general by the Continental Congress.

After Great Britain, France was the nation with which the American colonies were most directly concerned in 1776. But, under the influence of the Enlightenment, it was a time of change in general. Thus, events and movements in other parts of Europe, although of little immediate concern to America, were eventually to be of importance to the world, including the Western Hemisphere.

4

Europe

Four Enlightened Despots

As usual, the rise and fall of nations went steadily on in the latter part of the eighteenth century. For Europe in general it was a time of growth in population, in economic strength, and in learning and science.

To the east of France, the strongest of the older powers was Austria. Austria, as a domain under the Hapsburgs, consisted in 1776 of far more than the present-day nation of that name. It included Hungary, Belgium and parts of what are now Italy, Germany, Poland, Yugoslavia and Czechoslovakia. Austria itself had a population of about 6,000,000 and the capital city of this large and scattered empire, Vienna, had about 200,000.

The Hapsburgs, the ruling house of Austria since the thirteenth century, were also the rulers of the Holy Roman Empire, such as it was by the late eighteenth century. The Holy Roman Empire originated in the tenth century, stemming from the older Roman Empire and from the need for Christian unity in Europe against the Moslem invasions. Since 1438 the emperors had all been Hapsburgs and for practical purposes the position was hereditary. Supposedly, the Holy Roman Emperor was the supreme temporal ruler of Christendom, just as the Pope in Rome was the supreme spiritual ruler, but by this time the title had little real meaning.

In Austria, Maria Theresa (1717–80) was empress, but since a woman could not be Holy Roman Emperor, her son Joseph II (1741–90) held that title and ruled jointly with his mother over the wide array of people of many nationalities and languages. Maria Theresa became empress of Austria in 1740 and was a popular ruler, devoted to her work. She was also a very attractive and kind-hearted woman who had sixteen children, eleven of them daughters. Although somewhat conservative, Maria Theresa qualified as an enlightened despot and instituted many reforms, including the abolition of torture in her domains (except for Hungary) in 1776. She liberated the peasants from some of the remaining burdens of feudalism.

Joseph II, who became Holy Roman Emperor in 1765, had greater enthusiasm for reform than his mother, but used less common sense in applying his policies. He proclaimed reforms in taxation, the administration of justice and the regulation of trade; sought the removal of some of the burdensome rules of feudalism that still existed; furthered education; and, especially, took strong measures to make the church subject to state control. Joseph believed that a firmly run state could solve all problems and that he as ruler could speak for the state and its people. He could not try out all of his own ideas until after his mother's death in 1780. Then he found that different groups objected, for reasons of self-interest or habit, to many of his proposed changes.

Both Maria Theresa and Joseph were well served by

Wenzel Anton Kaunitz who was chancellor and foreign minister of Austria for almost forty years, from 1753 to 1792. He was the first in high office to see that Prussia, rather than France, had become the chief threat to Austria.

In the world of the arts, Austria was the home of two of the greatest composers, Franz Joseph Haydn (1732–1809) and Wolfgang Amadeus Mozart (1756–91). Haydn was musical director to the Esterhazy princes, an ancient Hungarian family. At Eisenstadt, the seat of the princes, he composed most of the music that made him the "father of the symphony." Mozart, who began performing in the courts of Europe when he was only six, was appointed concertmaster to the archbishop of Salzburg in 1771, but in 1776 he was seeking a position at court. Haydn and Mozart were the first important composers to write for the piano, which had been invented earlier in the century.

The reform-minded Joseph II thought the theater could be a powerful force in educating people to approve his policies. Accordingly, in 1776 he decreed that the Burgtheater in Vienna, which had been built in 1741, should become a national theater that would present only serious and uplifting dramas. As director he appointed Joseph von Sonnenfels (1733–1817), who shared Joseph's desire to reform the Austrian theater. Even though Joseph banished light theater to the suburbs of Vienna, it nevertheless thrived and remained popular, perhaps expressing the true spirit of the people.

The rapidly rising power in western Europe was Prussia. A small unit of geography and population, Prussia had been increasing its military and economic strength, and expanding its territories in the Germanic areas for several generations. A new king came to the throne in 1740 (the same year that Maria Theresa succeeded to power in Austria). By then, thanks to the previous sovereigns, Prussia had an efficient civil service and a professional army of high quality. Although Prussia was primarily a rural land, industry was growing and was encouraged, while the nobility was loyal to the crown and was active in the army and the government. During the second half of the eighteenth century, Prussia—by war, threats of war and diplomatic pressure—increased the territory under its control from 46,500 to 76,000 square miles and thereby more than doubled the population. Berlin, the capital, had a population of about 150,000.

Frederick II (1712–86), known now as Frederick the Great, was the ruler who, building on the spartan regimes of his two predecessors, made Prussia a major power in the course of the Age of Reason. Only twenty-eight years old, and having had a most unpleasant relationship with his boorish father, Frederick William I, Frederick came to the throne determined to do things his own way and to be an even more efficient ruler than his father. At the same time, along with the urge to expand his territories and to hold to old-fashioned mercantilist economic policies, Frederick wished to rule as a benevolent despot.

In proper Enlightenment terms, he thought of himself as "the first servant of the state." He did not live in elegant splendor as did the French monarchs, but wore old clothes and spent endless hours fussing over the details of government. He found solace in playing the flute, and intellectual stimulation in inviting to his court such men as Voltaire. He corresponded with other *philosophes.* Frederick ordered religious toleration, abolished serfdom on the royal estates, and reformed the criminal law and judicial procedures. The British ambassador to Prussia wrote, in March, 1776, that Frederick's character was a "motley composition of barbarity and humanity." Two months later, the hard-working but aging monarch noted that he had by then had eighteen attacks of the gout and was not in good health.

Two products of the Prussian military regime were to join

other European soldiers in America to fight alongside the colonists. Friedrich Wilhelm, Baron von Steuben (1730–94), fought in the Seven Years War for Prussia and in 1762 became an aide to Frederick. He played an important role in reforming and training the Prussian army but later fell out of favor with the king, at about the time the Revolution was beginning in America. While he was in Paris in 1777, he was persuaded to go to America to help train the Continental Army. Johann Kalb (1721–80), who assumed the title of Baron de Kalb to help his army career, also served in the Seven Years War, but in the French army. In 1768 he was sent to the colonies as a French secret agent, and in 1776, he, too, was recruited to fight for the Americans. Both Steuben and Kalb were with Washington and his army during the bitter winter at Valley Forge, 1777–78, and both greatly aided the American cause. Like Lafayette and others, they were recruited by Silas Deane (1737–89), who had been a member of the Continental Congress and who was sent to France in 1776 as the colonies' diplomatic agent.

In spite of the militaristic atmosphere that surrounded Frederick's rule, German philosophy and literature were second only to that of France. Immanuel Kant (1724–1804), one of the most influential philosophers of all time, spent his life in Konigsberg, East Prussia, where he was so regular in his habits that residents of the city are said to have set their watches by his daily walks. He was professor of logic and metaphysics there in 1776, holding the position for nearly thirty-five years in all and finally, in 1781, publishing his major work, the *Critique of Pure Reason*. His thought and writings embraced many moral and intellectual subjects, such as logic, ethics and religion.

Of equal stature was Johann Wolfgang von Goethe (1749–1832). In 1774, when he was only twenty-five, he achieved fame and great popularity with his novel, *The Sorrows of Werther*. Late in the next year he was invited to the duchy of

Weimar where he spent the rest of his life, during ten years of which he was chief minister of state to the duke of Saxe-Weimar. Goethe was a reformer but he opposed change that was too sudden or violent. He believed reform should come through the actions of the head of the state. He found time to write prolifically, including the drama, *Stella,* in 1776. For a great deal of his life he was at work on his two most famous works: *Wilheim Meister,* a novel of character development; and one of the world's notable poetic and philosophical works, the dramatic poem *Faust,* based on the legend of a man who sells his soul to the devil for the material world. Goethe, although more emotional and romantic than such men as Voltaire (he was influenced more by Rousseau), was a man of the Enlightenment in his outlook. He was not only a poet, dramatist and novelist, but also had a lifelong interest in biology and did research on animals and plants.

Other German contributors to the world of letters included Friedrich Grimm (1723–1807), Gotthold Ephraim Lessing (1729–81), Christoph Martin Wieland (1733–1813) and Johann Gottfried von Herder (1744–1803). Grimm lived a good deal of the time in France and wrote articles on music for the *Encyclopédie.* Lessing, a philosopher and dramatist as well as a critic, was one of the most influential figures of the Enlightenment, being its chief German exponent. His very successful play, *Miss Sara Sampson* (1755), a tragedy of domestic middle-class life, marked the beginning of modern German theater. From 1770 on, he was librarian to the duke of Brunswick at Wolfenbuttel, where he wrote a significant critical work on history and literature. Wieland, called by some the "German Voltaire," partly because of his fluent, elegant style, was tutor to the sons of the duke of Saxe-Weimar. Herder, a student of theology as well as a philosopher and poet, became court preacher at Weimar in 1776, thanks to Goethe's influence, and stayed there the remainder of his life.

In the music world, a German composer was the center of a lively controversy. Christoph Willibald von Gluck (1714–87), a Bavarian who spent most of his professional life in Vienna, reformed opera by giving greater unity in his compositions to the music and the text. This left less room for individual stars to show off their talents by doing as they pleased. Partly through the influence of Queen Marie Antoinette who had been his pupil, the Paris Opera commissioned Gluck to produce six operas. Thus it was that he was in Paris in 1776 at the time a French adaptation of his *Alceste* was performed. A great dispute arose between the followers of Gluck and those who did not like the new style in opera. The somewhat unwilling champion of the anti-Gluck faction was Niccolo Piccini (1728–1800), an Italian and the composer of more than a hundred operas, who happened to be in Paris at the time. Actually, Piccini admired Gluck.

Carl Philipp Emanuel Bach (1714–88), a son of Johann Sebastian Bach, spent twenty-eight years at the court of Frederick the Great where his chief duty was to accompany Frederick's flute on the harpsichord. He left the court in 1767 and in 1776 was in Hamburg where he directed music for the five leading churches of the city.

The eighteenth century saw the German theater become established as a permanent and important part of cultural life. Leading figures of the theatrical world were Konrad Ekhof (1720–78) and Friedrich Ludwig Schroeder (1744–1816). Ekhof, the founder of the realistic school of acting in Germany, did much to raise the status of actors. He had a wonderful voice which enabled audiences to forget that he was short and had a very plain face. Schroeder, probably the greatest name in German theatrical history, was influenced by Ekhof. He was also a fine actor and was the first manager to introduce Shakespeare to the German stage. He began such a series at the Hamburg Theater in 1776 with his adaptation of *Hamlet*—in which Hamlet did not die at the end.

Leonhard Euler (1707–83), who may have been the world's most prolific mathematician, was a Swiss who spent his professional life first in Russia, then in Berlin at the invitation of Frederick the Great, and later returned to Russia. One of the founders of higher mathematics, he was also an early explorer of the relation of music to mathematics. During the last seventeen years of his life, when he was at the court of Catherine the Great in St. Petersburg, Euler was blind but yet managed to turn out half of his total of 800 books and articles. Johann Elert Bode (1747–1826) was a German astronomer who was associated with the Academy of Science in Berlin for many years. In 1772 he devised a formula to express the relative distances of the planets from the sun.

Germany's leading eccentric was Franz Anton Mesmer (1733?–1815). A physician, he became interested in what he termed "animal magnetism." He developed a system of treatment using hypnosis, which came to be called "mesmerism." He refused to reveal the secret of his "magnetic cures" and eventually was prevented from practicing by a governmental investigation.

A little more than half a century before 1776, Russia had hardly been considered a European country. Then Emperor Peter the Great, before his death in 1725, brought Russia into contact with the West. He forced his nation to adopt Western ways and set Russia on the first steps toward becoming an important world power. Largely as a result of expanding her territory by military conquest, Russia was rapidly overtaking France in population and during the century grew from about 12,000,000 to 30,000,000 people.

Moscow was the largest city with a population of more than 200,000, followed by St. Petersburg which had not quite reached that figure.

In spite of efforts at Westernization, Russia was primarily a rural nation and nearly half the population consisted of serfs or peasants on state-owned lands. The gentry, although amounting to only one per cent of the population, dominated the life of the country. Nevertheless, in the course of the century, Russia moved from medieval times to the Age of Reason. After Peter the Great, the ruler most responsible for this change was the one who sat on the throne in 1776 and during whose reign Russia grew to be as powerful as any other nation on the Continent.

That ruler was the Empress Catherine the Great (1729–96), who became the czarina in 1762. Catherine, the daughter of a petty German prince, was brought to Russia when she was only fifteen to marry the heir to the throne. Early in 1762 her completely incompetent husband became Czar Peter III, but he soon aroused both hatred and contempt. A group opposed to him proclaimed Catherine ruler in June and soon thereafter Peter was murdered. Just what part Catherine herself played in this is not certain.

Catherine was assisted to the throne by Grigori Orlov (1734–83), who was one of the first of her many lovers. Catherine was apparently attractive to men, and they to her, although she was "inclined to grow corpulent," as one British observer wrote. She also used quite a bit of rouge. In any event, she had intelligence and ability and at the outset of her reign was determined to follow the ideals of the Enlightenment. In 1767 she called a national assembly which started out with instructions that might have led to rational reforms, but when the assembly seemed to be moving too quickly, and when war with Turkey became a more important matter, it was quietly disbanded.

Catherine's enthusiasm for reform dropped still further

as a result of the Pugachev rebellion which began in 1773. A nearly illiterate Cossack, Yemelyan Ivanovich Pugachev, set himself up as the leader of a peasant revolt. He played on the belief of some of the people that Peter III was still alive, and he claimed to be Peter. His movement grew and he became the leader of a formidable army of Cossacks, peasants and serfs which overran large areas in the lower Volga and Ural regions and captured some fortresses. The revolutionists were exceedingly barbarous and became a serious threat to the throne. Lack of experienced leadership eventually brought about the movement's downfall and early in 1775 Pugachev was betrayed, captured and executed. During this trying time Grigori Potemkin (1739–91) became Catherine's chief adviser and also her lover. He continued his governmental duties after others had taken his place among the empress's lovers. Catherine put through some reforms, such as encouraging trade by freeing it of internal restrictions, and promoted industrial development. Her educational reforms were noteworthy: she was a pioneer in providing education for girls, she established the first important teacher-training program in Russia and she opened schools in many places where they had not existed. On the other hand, she allowed the gentry to strengthen their hold over the serfs, freed the nobles of taxation and instituted other administrative measures which were reactionary rather than enlightened. On balance, there is some question as to whether she deserved to be called an enlightened despot. In any event, she read the *philosophes,* invited Diderot to visit her, which he did, and corresponded with Voltaire.

Russian writers also felt the influence of the Enlightenment and, as in other countries, some of them ran into trouble for opposing the government. Nikolai Novikov (1744–1818) was a satirist who had published three different periodicals by 1776. His jibes at society kept getting him into difficulties. The most important work of Alexander

Radishchev (1749–1802) did not appear until 1790 and it caused him to be jailed, probably because he was influenced by the French thinkers. Gavril Derzhavin (1743–1816), the best of Russia's poets of the century, was not a rebel. He became poet laureate because Catherine liked his semi-humorous ode to her.

The Russian theater prospered, influenced by the French and German theaters. Catherine herself wrote plays which were performed. Theater as an important aspect of cultural life in Russia was quite new. The father of Russian drama, who wrote the first classical tragedy in Russian in 1747, was near the end of his career. He was Alexander Sumarkov (1718–77) who some years before had been dismissed as head of the Russian theater because of his too-liberal views. The major dramatist now was Denis Fonvizin (1745–92) whose first work, a translation, was produced when he was only eighteen. He was a satirist, as in his play, *The Brigadier-General* (1766), which made fun of the crude, newly rich men then trying to enter Russian society. He wrote in the comic style current in France, but he introduced elements of Russian folk comedy. One of the first actors of importance was Ivan Dmitrevsky (1733–1821) who in 1776 held the highest post in the St. Petersburg Theater, where he ruled as both actor and manager. A very gifted actor, he played both comic and tragic parts equally well. Better educated than actors usually were at that time, Dmitrevsky wrote and translated plays and compiled a history of the Russian theater.

While France, Austria, Prussia and Russia could determine the course of events on the Continent, other states, some ascending, others no longer as powerful as they had once been, were also affected by the Enlightenment.

5

And Some Others

From Poland westward to Spain, and from Italy northward to Scandinavia, a variety of kingdoms, duchies and city-states filled out the Continent. For several of them, their days of greatest glory were past, while others were to see better times in the future.

Poland, because of its own backwardness and also because of its geographical position, was at the mercy of Russia, Austria and Prussia. These three powers had partly dismantled Poland in 1772, Russia taking territory in eastern Poland, Prussia raiding on the west and Austria on the south. Poland's backwardness extended from its peasants, among the most wretched anywhere, to its nobles, described by one historian as "rude, slovenly, uneducated and provincial." They were almost untouched by the rest of the world, including the currents of the Enlightenment. The kingship of Poland was elective and it was not always easy to get agreement on a candidate. In the legislature, controlled by the nobles, one vote could defeat any proposal, dissolve the parliament and set aside all laws already passed.

The king of this unmanageable land in 1776 was Stanislaus II (1732–98), or Stanislaus Poniatowski before his election in 1764. He had been one of Catherine the Great's lovers while he was Polish ambassador to Russia, and he was imposed on Poland as king by Catherine and Frederick the Great. Stanislaus was the last king of Poland.

Poland had some men of prominence in intellectual fields. Among them was Hugon Kollataj (1750–1812) who, beginning in 1776 when he was only twenty-six, was active in attempts at educational and governmental reform. Stanislaw Staszyc (1755–1826) was also a reformer and studied in Paris under Buffon. Poland's most distinguished writer of the Enlightenment was Ignacy Krasicki (1735–1801), who was trained for the church and became a bishop at the age of thirty-one. He wrote satires, comic epics, novels, fables and poetry.

Two Polish military men became such enthusiastic supporters of the American Revolution that they, too, like the Frenchman Lafayette, journeyed to the colonies and offered their services. Thaddeus Kosciusko (1746–1817) arrived in America in 1776, became a colonel of engineers, and served the following year in the Saratoga campaign, as well as in later battles. Casimir Pulaski (1748–1779) had to flee Poland in 1772 because of his part in an unsuccessful rebellion against Stanislaus II. He was in France when the events in America, such as the adoption of the Declaration of Independence, led him to decide to join the colonists. He arrived in America in 1777, was commissioned a brigadier general, and served with distinction until fatally wounded in a cavalry charge in 1779.

Spain, once one of the leading powers on the Continent, no longer held that place except so far as its enormous New World colonies gave it a unique position in world affairs.

Spain was recovering from past disasters, including having been on the losing side in the Seven Years War. Population was increasing but was somewhat under 10,000,000.

The progress in Spain during this period was due largely to the efforts of another of the enlightened despots. He was Charles III (1716–88) of the house of Bourbon, who succeeded his half-brother, Ferdinand VI, in 1759. Charles was intelligent, a patron of the arts and an efficient monarch. He improved the administration of the Spanish colonies, encouraged economic development at home and fostered better schools. As was usually the case, he ran into opposition from various groups that didn't want to have to change their ways. In South America a continuing dispute with Portugal over the area of Rio de la Plata basin, where southern Brazil and Spanish colonial territory met, caused Spain to go to war against its neighbor in 1776. The fighting took place in South America and was resolved the next year before spreading.

A young man who was to become one of the most admired artists of all time was just starting his career in Madrid. Francisco Goya (1746–1828) returned to Madrid in 1775 after studying in Rome. The following year he began work on a series of tapestry designs which were produced by the royal tapestry factory. Goya's work, gay and romantic in spirit and brilliant in every respect, caught the attention of the king. An outstanding poet at a time when there was not much good Spanish poetry was Juan Melendez Valdes (1754–1817), who wrote in the neo-classical style and was influenced by the French.

Portugal, too, had known a period of greater splendor and could no longer count as a major power except that it possessed the huge land of Brazil. Portugal was also ruled by an enlightened monarch who approached his problems much as did Charles III of Spain. He was Joseph I (1714–77), who was king from 1750 until his death. In practice, his chief minister the Marques de Pombal (1699–1782) exercised at least as much power as the king. Slavery was ended in Portugal, the Indians in Brazil were emancipated and steps were taken to encourage commerce.

Italy, as a national state, did not exist. Instead the land was carved up into a large number of minor kingdoms, duchies and city-states, among them Naples, Parma, Milan, Savoy, Tuscany, Venice, Genoa and Mantua. The Austrian Hapsburgs dominated many of the small states, while the Spanish Bourbons had influence in others. Italy was at peace, and a number of duchies were ruled by benevolent despots who adopted the same pattern of reform as their more powerful counterparts. Reforms were needed, for while there were some extremely rich people, there were great numbers of Italians who were very, very poor.

Italy did influence and make contributions to the world of culture. Vittorio Alfieri (1749–1803) wrote tragedies in verse on classical, biblical and other themes. He attempted to revive a national spirit in Italy. Beginning in 1776 he wrote nineteen tragedies in the course of the next ten years, one of which he dedicated to George Washington. Another drama-tist, Carlo Goldoni (1707–93), reformed Italian comedy by writing out the dialogue in full instead of leaving it to be partly extemporaneous. He lived in Paris from 1761 on, where he wrote some of his 150 plays. Cesare Beccaria (1738–94), a criminologist, economist and jurist, stimulated penal reform by his writings and was one of the first to agitate against capital punishment.

Italy also contributed two eminent rascals and swash-bucklers, Giovanni Casanova (1725–98) and the Count Alessandro Cagliostro (1743–95), whose real name was Giuseppe Balsamo. Casanova, remembered today chiefly for his amorous adventures, visited many countries and was at different times a gambler, a spy, an author and a diplomat. He knew Voltaire, Catherine and Frederick. His memoirs give a vivid picture of eighteenth-century manners and morals as seen by a "jet-setter" of the time. Cagliostro was a less likable scoundrel. He, too, traveled widely, partly as did Casanova to escape from the authorities, and in 1776 he visited England. He duped many people with his claims as a magician and alchemist. Cagliostro said he possessed the "philosopher's stone," an imaginary substance that supposedly turned all metals into gold, and also an elixir of youth.

The popes of the Roman Catholic Church were temporal rulers over some of the lands of Italy, as well as spiritual heads of the church. Their power at this point was not very great in either realm. The nations on the rise were non-Catholic countries—Russia, Prussia, Great Britain and the American colonies—and even in such Catholic lands as Austria and Spain, secular rulers were at odds with the pope. Joseph II, for example, wanted to reform the church in Austria, appoint the clergy and suppress some of the monasteries. The pope to whom the task fell of trying to contain the enlightened despots and the secularism of the Enlightenment was Pius VI (1717–99), who was a cardinal for only about a year before being elected pope in 1775.

Greece, whose ancient culture inspired the neo-classicists, was itself almost nonexistent in the Age of Reason. Greece was under the rule of the Ottoman Empire and had not been free for centuries. Its people were obscure and extremely poor. A halfhearted rebellion in 1770 was given assistance by Catherine of Russia. She sent a small fleet to support the uprising, but after the fleet captured one port the rebels were defeated and gave up the fight.

Sweden had been counted among the major powers until worn down by too much warfare with Russia at about the start of the century. Now Sweden, too, had an enlightened despot, influenced by French thought, and seemed content to find a place among its neighbors proportionate to its strength. Gustav III (1746–92) became king in 1771. The next year, in a popular move, he carried out a coup that restored almost absolute power to the monarchy after a half-century of rule by legislative bodies. Gustav had charm and was liked by his subjects. He put through a number of governmental reforms and sponsored a cultural boom. Gustav was especially interested in the theater and was a poet and playwright himself. He performed in as well as wrote several plays which he had produced in the palace of Drottningholm. He supported the National Theater, which was established in 1773, and encouraged young dramatists.

Carl Michael Bellman (1740–95) and Johan Henrik Kellgren (1751–95) were the leading poets of the period. Bellman sometimes set his own verses to music. A protégé of the king, he was given an easy job in 1776 in connection with the state lottery. Kellgren was for a time librarian and secretary to the king, and his poetry expressed the ideas of the Enlightenment writers. He was also a playwright. Typical of Swedish artists of the period was Carl Gustaf Pilo (1711–93) who, like his fellow painters, spent quite a bit of time abroad in the course of his career. In Copenhagen, Denmark, he became a successful portrait painter. He returned to Sweden in 1772 and at his death left a huge unfinished painting of the coronation of Gustav III.

Carolus Linnaeus (1707–78), who took the name of Carl von Linné when he was ennobled, achieved international recognition as a botanist. He developed a system for classifying plants and animals, and although his system was later revised and improved, his work increased the accuracy of descriptions of flora and fauna.

Christian VII (1749–1808), who ruled the united kingdom of Denmark and Norway from 1766 to his death, brought reforms to his part of Scandinavia. The king was mentally ill some of the time, and so much of the actual government fell into the hands of Andreas Peter Bernstoff (1735–99). Among their reforms was the freeing of the serfs.

Under French and British influence, poetry and drama in the neo-classical style flourished, while German influence could also be seen in the work of some of the Danish and Norwegian poets. Johannes Ewald (1743–81) as a child had tried to run away in order to imitate Robinson Crusoe. He later served as a volunteer in the Prussian army in the Seven Years War, and eventually became the leading Danish poet and playwright. He helped revive interest in Scandinavian mythology and wrote the first original Danish tragedy, *Rolf Krage,* in 1770. His operetta of 1779, *The Fishermen,* contained the song "King Christian Stood by the Lofty Mast," which became the Danish national anthem.

The Dutch in the Netherlands no longer held the position of power they had enjoyed when their navy was one of the strongest in the world and they were competing with Great Britain and others in the scramble for colonies in America and the Far East. With a population of less than 2,000,000, of whom about ten per cent lived in Amsterdam, the Dutch retained an important position in international trade and finance. Banking flourished and a good deal of the national debt of Great Britain was held by the Dutch.

Dutch art and literature were both in a period of decline in the late eighteenth century compared with previous times. This was caused, at least in part, by the popularity and influence of French styles and the French language. Elisabeth Wolff (1738–1804), author of satirical articles and poems, collaborated with Agatha Deken (1741–1804) to write some very popular and sentimental novels. Art was decorative, in keeping with tastes of the time. Aert Schouman (1710–92) was a versatile artist who produced everything from wallpaper designs to engravings on glass. His best work consisted of watercolors of birds and animals.

The nations of Europe, large and small, were all of some interest or importance to the Americans and the events taking shape in North America. Most of the rest of the world did not seem so relevant.

6

The Middle East and Africa

Ottoman Turks and Black Slaves

South of Europe and far to the east of America lay two areas that differed vastly from Western civilization. Geographically, this part of the world consists of the Middle East (all that extension of the continent of Asia westward from Afghanistan and Pakistan) and the continent of Africa. For practical purposes, because of religious, historical and ethnic factors, the area divides into two parts in a somewhat different way: the Middle East and the northern part of Africa on the one hand; Africa south of the Sahara Desert—that is, Black Africa—on the other.

Almost the entire Asian and North African area was under the control of the empire of the Ottoman Turks, successors to the earlier Arabic rulers. This empire, the result of the spread of the Islamic religion, began in the early seventh century when Mohammed, the founder of Islam, developed and expanded both religious and territorial rule out of Arabia where, in the city of Mecca, he first proclaimed the new faith. The Ottoman Turks began their conquests in the thirteenth century, and by the early sixteenth century they dominated the Arabic and Islamic world. Their capital was Constantinople (now Istanbul), the former chief city of the eastern Roman Empire, with a population of about 600,000. The territory of the Turks reached its greatest extent in the late seventeenth century. At that time the Ottoman Empire took in not only Asia Minor, Iraq, Syria, Palestine, Egypt and the North African coast, but also a good deal of southeastern Europe, including Hungary and territory almost to the gates of Vienna. The Ottoman realm stretched from the Atlantic Ocean to the Persian Gulf.

Now, under outside pressure from Austria and Russia and plagued with revolts within, the Ottoman Empire was decaying. In some quarters this was blamed on the alleged corruption of the original teachings of Mohammed. One response to this was a movement that started in central Arabia and was led by Mohammed ibn Abdul Wahhab (1703–92), who preached that Islam must be cleansed and purified.

In Egypt, home of one of the most ancient of civilizations, Turkish rule had declined greatly by the late eighteenth century. In the early sixteenth century the Ottomans established their power in Egypt by defeating the Mameluke rulers. The Mamelukes were men of a warrior caste whose beginnings could be traced all the way back to the tenth century when slaves of non-Arabic ethnic stock had been trained to serve as warriors. By 1250 they had grown strong enough to take control of the government of Egypt. Now they were doing so again and by 1776 the Mamelukes were once more the real rulers of Egypt. A little earlier, in northern Palestine, Dahir al Omar, with help from Egypt and Russia, established an almost independent area in defiance of the Turks. He was defeated and killed in 1775 so that in

1776 the region was ruled by a nominee of the Ottomans —
Ahmed Pasha Jazzar, known as "The Butcher."

Still farther east, the Persians invaded Basra, one of the
Iraqi provinces of the Ottoman Empire, and after a long
siege forced the city to surrender in April, 1776. Persia (now
Iran) was divided between two dynasties. In the western
and southern area Karim Khan, founder of the Zand
dynasty, ruled from 1750 to 1779. He made Shiraz his capital
and constructed there lavish palaces, gardens and mosques.
In the eastern part of the country, the Afshar dynasty held
sway. The ruler was Shak Rukh, a blind son of the previous
king, who reigned from 1748 to 1796. In the early eighteenth
century Persia invaded its neighbor on the east, Afghanistan; but after the Persian conqueror died in 1747, one of
his lieutenants, Ahmed Shah, put himself in power and
began the Durand dynasty. He, in turn, was succeeded by
his son who ruled Afghanistan from 1773 to 1793 when he
died, leaving twenty-three sons.

South of the Sahara Desert lay an entirely different world.
A great deal of it was equatorial in climate. The inhabitants
were Black, although not otherwise all the same genetically
by any means. Organized society was more comparable
with medieval Europe than with the eighteenth century. Of
all the continents, Africa was the last to feel the full impact
of European civilization, and few attempts at colonization
or even at colonial rule were attempted until the nineteenth
century. The white man knew only the coastline and was
almost completely ignorant of what the interior of Africa
contained. Nevertheless, Africa in the age of the Enlightenment was of great economic importance to Europe because
of commerce in its products — gold, ivory and, above all,
slaves.

Unique among the states of Africa was Ethiopia, occupy-
ing an area in the northeastern part of the continent, east
of the Sudan and south of Egypt. Ever since the Ethiopian

rulers had been converted from paganism in the fourth century, the country had been officially Christian, but it was later cut off from most of its religious contacts by the Islamic conquest of North Africa. In the eighteenth century Ethiopia's form of Christianity was that of the Coptic Church, a term which came originally from the Copts of Egypt—a group of people who remained Christian when most Egyptians were turning to Islam. The Ethiopian Coptic Church differed with the Church in Europe and Asia on certain matters of belief—for example, whether Jesus Christ had two natures, human and divine, or only one, divine—and so the Ethiopians had few ties with the rest of Christianity. For Ethiopia, the latter part of the eighteenth century was a time of trouble. Governors of the various provinces fought for supremacy, because the power and prestige of the ruling monarchy had been declining for some time. It was, indeed, a century of upheaval, with the situation so confused, and with would-be leaders contending for power to such an extent, that by 1800 no fewer than six different "emperors" were being pushed forward by one chieftain or another.

The impact of Black Africa and white Europe and America on each other in the eighteenth century occurred chiefly in the west-central area of the continent. Most closely tied to the New World was that part of the coast which runs largely east and west, rather than north and south, from present-day Nigeria to the Ivory Coast, around the Gulf of Guinea.

Many kingdoms rose and fell in this general area over the centuries. The kingdom of the Congo, for example, with its northern boundary at the Congo River, held sway over extensive territory when the Portuguese first arrived in the late fifteenth century. But by the late eighteenth century its power was collapsing. The strongest kingdom in the southeastern Congo was that of the Baluba (in what later became Katanga and Kivu provinces) which was established in the sixteenth century and lasted until well into the nineteenth.

To the north and west of the Congo, in what is now Nigeria, the Benin kingdom, one of the most powerful political systems in western Africa in its heyday, was a large empire held together by the emperor's prestige. Founded in the fifteenth century, it lasted into the nineteenth, but was declining in the late eighteenth. Rich in trade, it also produced some of the finest art of Africa—iron work, bronze portrait busts and carved ivory. In addition, Benim permitted slavery and made use of human sacrifices on ceremonial occasions.

In what is now Ghana, the Ashanti was the strongest kingdom on the west coast. Having defeated other states, it was at the height of its power and, as the Romans did, ruled its conquered areas through proconsuls. Ivory, gold and slaves provided the bulk of a rich trade for this nation, too. Along the Ivory Coast, and in various other areas, there were still other Black kingdoms whose contacts with the Europeans changed forever their history.

From this middle section of western Africa—one part of the coastland was known as the Slave Coast—came the mass of Black slaves who made Africa one of the focal points of interest for Europe and America alike all through the century. The slave trade and the age of Enlightenment were at their height at the same time. The business of exporting African slaves to the New World began in the early sixteenth century and expanded steadily. The growing European market for sugar and other agricultural products of the new lands fueled the demand for more cheap labor. The Portuguese, Dutch, French, Spaniards and British all engaged in the slave trade, but the British controlled over half of it. The best estimate of the traffic in the eighteenth century indicates that over 6,000,000 men, women and children were shipped off to slavery.

The slave trade could not exist without the participation

of African traders and rulers. The captains of the European slaveships brought merchandise with which to buy slaves — firearms, gin, cloth and metal goods. At first, many of those who were sold as slaves to the white men had already been slaves in Africa, usually as a result of having been captured in war. As the demand increased, this was not an adequate source of supply. Accordingly, some Black traders and rulers on the coast undertook to capture slaves in the interior, or even in some cases to sell their own tribesmen. The larger states and tribes were able to beat off most slave raids, but weaker groups were invaded regularly. In another part of Africa an example of the arrangement was summed up in an agreement signed in 1776 between a French trader and a ruler. The ruler, as middleman, promised to deliver a thousand slaves a year, and he was to keep a tenth of the purchase price for his services.

Along the west African coast, at such places as Elmina, Christianborg and Fort Metal Cross, the Europeans erected what came to be called "slave castles," but might more aptly be termed warehouses for storing human beings. Here, in dungeon-like quarters, slaves brought to the coast were held under miserable conditions until they were loaded on ships for the long journey to the New World. Great numbers of the slaves, jammed into the ships under frightful living conditions, died on the way to America. These slave castles also served as forts and headquarters for the Europeans.

Portugal for many years centered its efforts on Angola in southwest Africa. The powerful kingdom of the Lunda, the center of whose realm was well inland, cooperated with the Portuguese in securing slaves, and Angola was the source for most of the Blacks shipped to Brazil. The slaves from this area were considered among the best for plantation work in the New World.

While the slave trade created large-scale commercial dealings between Europe and Africa, the white nations made almost no attempts to colonize Africa as they had the Western Hemisphere until the nineteenth century. The one exception was in South Africa, where the Dutch East India Company founded Cape Town in 1652. It was intended as a supply station but by 1776 Dutch colonists were spreading out into the interior and were farming under frontier conditions. French, German and Scandinavian immigrants joined the Dutch as permanent settlers. Cape Town by now had a population of nearly 20,000.

About the same time that European contacts with Africa were increasing, the largest continent of all, Asia, was also feeling the impact of Western civilization.

7

Asia

An Old New World

While exploring and colonizing North and South America for nearly three centuries, the European nations were at the same time probing the very different lands of Asia. Here there existed civilizations older than that of western Europe, civilizations which were not eager to be Westernized. The Europeans found this hard to believe and moved aggressively to open up trade with these oriental lands or, in some cases, to conquer them. Thus far in the eighteenth century, trade with Asia had not been as important as that with the Western Hemisphere. Such countries as India, China and Japan did not provide large markets for Western goods. The Europeans, though, found many Asian goods to their liking, such as spices, silk, tea, drugs and porcelain. These had to be paid for, usually with gold or silver, and so this trade drained precious metals from Europe.

India lay open to European exploitation because, unlike

China and Japan, there was no strong central government. The Mogul Empire, which was Islamic, lost control early in the century. It continued to exist in name and Shah Alam II (1728–1806) claimed the throne from 1759 until his death. He exercised no real power and he turned over such authority as he had in Bengal to the British, in return for a pension. Many Hindu principalities were joined in a loose confederation, but more and more the British took over the real power.

Great Britain's victory in the Seven Years War, which ended in 1763, forced the French out of India and, as in North America, left the British with a clear field. They had been active in India for nearly two centuries, ever since Queen Elizabeth I chartered the British East India Company in 1600. As the company grew it became a political as well as a commercial force. In 1744 Parliament—wanting to have a say in the political affairs of India and wishing to secure some of the company's profits—assumed joint control. Calcutta in Bengal was made the seat of government and for the first time the British appointed a governor general for India.

Warren Hastings (1732–1818) was the man named to the new post and he held it until 1785. He was thus the first real ruler of British India. Hastings initially went to India in 1750 as a seventeen-year-old clerk for the East India Company. Working himself up in rank by his ability and his zeal, he was transferred from Madras to Bengal in 1772 to sort out the company's affairs, which were not then well managed. Hastings, who took the trouble to learn Urdu, Bengali and Arabic, set out to reform the business and legal administration of India. He codified laws and strengthened civil control. While he sternly put down native revolts and was high-handed in his methods, he was not corrupt as some other British officials had been. For some time many of Hastings's efforts were thwarted by his advisory council, a majority of which was hostile to him. The death of one of the anti-Hastings members in September, 1776, enabled the governor general henceforth to run things his way.

The eighteenth century—with Hindu elements battling the declining Mogul power, and the British waging war against various native states—did not provide a favorable atmosphere for the arts in India. Of interest because of its unusual style was a type of painting known as Rajput, for the area of northwest India in which it originated. Rajput painting was influenced by the Islamic tradition which the Moguls brought to India, but developed into a Hindu art form. Its subject matter came from Hindu legend, chiefly from the histories of the god Krishna. No great stress was put on technical perfection and colors were used in brilliant profusion. Between 1740 and 1785 especially, a large number of beautiful miniatures of Krishna were produced. They featured slender, elongated human figures and forests full of birds and animals. The decorative arts flourished as in the past in spite of political and military conflict. Gold necklaces and bracelets, elaborate jewel boxes and daggers with intricately worked gold and enamel handles were turned out for the royal and wealthy classes.

The Chinese Empire presented a far different face to the European traders and adventurers than did India. One of the most advanced countries in the world, China puzzled the Europeans because it did not welcome them, and it was therefore difficult for them to understand the way of life. The Ch'ing dynasty had held the throne of China since 1644, when the Manchus completed their conquest by capturing Peking. The Manchus were an alien frontier tribe who came from what is now Manchuria. Under their rule China entered one of its great ages and the Ch'ing dynasty controlled an expanded empire that enjoyed internal peace. China's population was about 250,000,000 people, and about 125,000,000 acres of land were under cultivation.

China had not yet felt the impact of the European Industrial Revolution and was primarily an agrarian country. Nevertheless, industrial capitalism was developing slowly on its own. In Nanking 30,000 looms for weaving silk were in operation. In the chinaware manufacturing center of Chingtechen, hundreds of privately owned kilns employed several hundred thousand workers. Salt and iron mining were well developed.

Since the Chinese thought of other people as barbarians who had nothing to offer China, it is perhaps not surprising that they showed no eagerness to expand commercial relations. For many years Canton was the only port foreigners were allowed to use for trading purposes, and all business transactions were closely regulated. Chinese tea accounted for most of the exports to England.

Ch'ien-lung (1711–99) ruled over the splendor of China as the fourth Manchu emperor. He ascended the throne in 1736, well-trained for his job and possessed of energy and ambition. Under him, China reached its greatest geographical limits, and dominated Southeast Asia. Already forty years on the throne and now sixty-five years old, Ch'ien-lung was beginning to exhibit some erratic judgments. He took a liking to a handsome young member of his bodyguard, Ho-shen, and promoted him to high positions. When Ho-shen was executed in 1799, after Ch'ien-lung's death, he was found to have plundered the state on such a grand scale that his property was worth nearly $1,500,000,000.

Ch'ien-lung prided himself on his interest in scholarship and the arts. He invited famous scholars to join his government and sponsored a literary project which resulted in the compilation of 36,000 volumes of works in history, the Chinese classics, philosophy and belles-lettres. The emperor took the occasion to remove anything that sounded anti-Manchu. All in all, Ch'ien-lung can properly be compared with such enlightened despots of Europe as Catherine the

Great and Frederick the Great. He summed up his attitude toward that part of the world, though, when he wrote King George III that China "possessed all things in abundance and had no need of manufactures of outside barbarians."

In spite of China's indifference to the West, a vogue for the Chinese style in decoration began in Europe early in the century and lasted for nearly a hundred years. *Chinoiserie* —decorative articles produced under the influence of Chinese art—affected styles in Great Britain and France especially. Chinese lacquers and porcelains were imported and then copied. Whole rooms were furnished in the Chinese manner, and in France chinoiserie was blended with the rococo style. No other nation of Asia affected Europe in this way.

Chinese art in the Ch'ing period achieved a high level of competence, especially in some of the applied arts such as ceramics. Color in porcelain was used more extensively than in the past, and Ch'ing artisans produced fine imitations of earlier ceramics. In the seventeenth and eighteenth centuries a number of Chinese artists, to whom the term "Individualists" was later applied, revolted against the traditional styles in painting and brought a more spontaneous expression into their work. Their brushwork was rough compared with the precise style of the traditionalists, and their paintings were less stylized than the official schools preferred. The Individualists' influence was felt by nineteenth-century Japanese painters as well as by Chinese artists. In part, their "revolt" stood out simply because reverence was so strong in China. One group was centered in the city of Yangchow, which was noted for its brilliant social and cultural life. These men became known as the "Eight Eccentrics of Yangchow," and two of them were still alive in 1776—Min Chèn and Lo P'ing (1733–99). Lo P'ing painted delicate studies of flowers, birds and insects, such as "Wasps and Brambles" and "Dragonfly and

Poppy." He often lettered some of his own highly literary poems on his paintings.

The foremost intellectual was Tai Chen (1724–77), considered the greatest scholar and thinker of the whole Ch'ing dynasty that lasted for over 250 years. Tai was a doubter who sought evidence before accepting any statement. He said: "Having an inaccurate understanding of ten [things] is worth less than having a true understanding of one." The most highly praised poet of the time was Yüan Mei (1716–97), who liked to live well and admitted it. He represented in literature the same refusal to abide by customary standards as did the Individualist painters in art. He refused to let his poetic inspiration be restricted by what was generally considered proper literary style and usage.

In Korea the Yi dynasty had held sway since 1392, and had built a new capital at Seoul. In practice, though, Korea was a vassal state of China for more than a century and was not permitted to have contact with the outside world. Internally, Korea was misgoverned most of the time by upper-class officials, many of whom were corrupt.

In the area of Southeast Asia that now includes such nations as Burma, Thailand, Cambodia, North and South Vietnam, Laos, Malaysia, Indonesia and the Philippine Islands, there was a great deal of shifting of power and of territorial control in the eighteenth century, as small dynasties warred with each other. Some of these dynasties and kingdoms differed from their neighbors ethnically, culturally or linguistically. Among the groups were the Burmese, Thai, Mon, Khmer, Cham and Annamese. In other cases, rival families contended for power within kingdoms. Chinese influence had shaped the culture in some parts of Southeast Asia, in others Indian influence predominated. Islam and Christianity helped determine the destiny of certain areas, such as Indonesia and the Philippines.

Burma was ruled by the Alaungpaya dynasty, established in 1752 by a minor official of that name who defeated the Mon kingdom. Alaungpaya died in 1760 after having made Rangoon the Burmese capital city. Several of his successors tried in vain to conquer Siam. In the world of letters, Let-we-Thon-dara was a Burmese court minister and poet who wrote in the years between 1752 and 1783.

Siam (Thailand) was considered by seventeenth-century Europeans the most important kingdom in Southeast Asia. It seemed to be more stable and developed than neighboring nations. The French sent troops to Siam in 1687, presumably to keep the British out, but actually there was a plot to seize the kingdom and put it under French domination. When the plot was discovered, some of the princes and government ministers revolted and forced the French to withdraw. This anti-foreign reaction was so strong that Siam was then closed to outsiders for more than a century. General Phya Tak was near the end of a successful ten-year effort in 1776 to drive the Burmese from his country.

In turn, Cambodia, to the east and south, lost three western provinces to Siam during the century, and war and intrigue were prevalent well into the nineteenth century. Cochin China, the southern region of present-day South Vietnam, was infiltrated by the Annamese from the next region north. The Annamese, a people of Mongolian descent closely related to the Chinese, had for centuries been the dominant ethnic group in both parts of Vietnam. At first the invasion of the Cochin China area, which was then ruled by the Khmer, was commercial in nature; but by the mid-eighteenth century the Annamese controlled the country's government as well. Farther north in Vietnam, the Le dynasty was the ruling house, but within the kingdom powerful family groups fought for power and territory. For example, the Trinh family captured the cities of Hué and Hanoi in 1776 from the Tay Son group.

In the islands of Indonesia, especially on Java, the Dutch emerged in the early seventeenth century as the controlling power. Under the management of the Dutch East India Company, this control expanded steadily in the eighteenth century. Agriculture was developed to provide more goods for export.

The Philippine Islands, of all parts of Southeast Asia, were most directly under European control. Spanish explorers touched at the Philippines as early as 1521. Administrators and Catholic clergymen brought Western law and Christianity to some of the many islands. For a long time the Chinese had been emigrating to the Philippines in large numbers. They aroused antagonism on the islands that broke out into violent action periodically, because they controlled much of the local business. Every so often they were ordered expelled, or were massacred in large numbers, or both. One of the years when all Chinese were told to get out was 1776.

Europe and Japan had had some contact since the mid-sixteenth century, but two centuries later they still knew little about each other. Some trade had taken place, and Christianity had been introduced to Japan as well as Western learning. In theory Japan was ruled by an autocratic emperor, but in practice the actual power since the twelfth century had been exercised by the shogun. Originally, shogun was the title of the commander of the emperor's army, but gradually powerful families made the shogunate hereditary until displaced by another family, and a succession of such families ruled Japan. The Tokugawa family secured supreme power in 1603 and held the shogunate until 1867.

Tokugawa rule brought both internal and external peace to Japan, under a harsh centralized feudalism, at a time when Europe was devastated by religious and dynastic warfare. Yedo (later named Tokyo) was made the capital and grew from a small town to a population of nearly a million by

1800. The shogunate kept the warrior class, the samurai, under control, and made use of it in ruling. A new merchant class grew up but it was still insecure in relation to the rest of society. A "floating world" of entertainers, actors, writers, artists and "cafe society," devoted to the popular arts, pleasure and the bohemian life, added a touch of glamour to Japanese civilization.

After nearly 175 years of power, the Tokugawa Shogunate was past its prime. One of the descendants of the first shogun of the family now held the title: Ieshige, who ruled from 1745 to 1788. He was rather stupid and had such a bad stammer that almost no one could understand him. His favorite samurai interpreted for him, which gave the favorite a great deal of power.

The well-regulated atmosphere of the Tokugawa period encouraged writers, and literary production was large in quantity and high in quality. But, like the shogunate itself, literary quality was declining. Taniguchi Buson (1716–83) added refinements to the traditional seventeen-syllable verse form, the *haiku;* Karai Senryū (1717–90) parodied the *haiku;* while Yokoi Yayu (1701–83) wrote in a new form, a kind of *haiku* in prose. A novelist of the time was Ueda Akinari (1734–1809), whose best work, *Tales of the Rainy Moon* appeared in 1768. This was a collection of stories based on Japanese and Chinese sources. Turning from literature, he spent most of the next twelve years working in the field of medicine.

Japanese art enjoyed its last period of greatness in the Tokugawa era, drawing inspiration both from Chinese art, which had long been influential, and from European art, although not too much of the latter entered Japan. Yosa Buson (1716–83) worked under considerable Chinese influence. One of his paintings, "Crested Mynah Birds in a Plum Tree," was completed in 1776. It now hangs in the Freer Gallery of Art on Jefferson Drive in Washington, D.C.

Ikeno Taiga (1723–76), another painter of the same school as Yosa Buson, was an excellent calligrapher and was the first artist to earn a living by selling painted fans. Maruyama Okyo (1733–95) founded a school of painting that bore his name. These painters combined the Chinese style with a certain naturalism which they had learned from European art.

In extreme contrast with the ancient civilizations of China and Japan were the continent of Australia and the islands of New Zealand, thinly populated only by their aboriginal inhabitants. Lying far south in the Pacific Ocean, they had been only sketchily visited and mapped by Europeans. Both lands were "discovered" in the early sixteenth century to the extent that they were sighted by one or more explorers who had no idea what sort of land they were gazing upon.

The intrepid Captain James Cook (1728–79), on a voyage which took him around the world exploring various lands for Great Britain, saw New Zealand in 1769. The next year he landed in Australia at Botany Bay, near the present city of Sydney, and took possession of a land whose extent he did not know, in the name of George III. He sailed up the east coast on his way around the world. Cook, who also demonstrated that the dread disease of scurvy could be prevented by enforcing a diet of vegetables and fruit on his crews, began his last exploration on July 12, 1776, when he sailed from Plymouth, England. His purpose this time was to seek a northwest sea passage from the Pacific to the Atlantic. On his return voyage in 1779 he was killed by natives during a stopover in the Hawaiian Islands.

The energetic, aggressive Europeans were busily probing at all parts of the world, and the one area not yet discussed — South and Central America — was no exception. Here, unlike most of the rest of the world where the British were ahead in the race for colonies and trade, the Spanish and the Portuguese still held sway.

8

Latin America
Empire on a Grand Scale

With the exceptions of Guiana on the northeast coast of South America and some of the West Indian islands, the story of Latin America — and of extensive parts of the future United States — in the eighteenth century is the story of the overseas empires of two European nations, Spain and Portugal. Here the conquest and colonization of the New World began earlier than along the coast of North America.

The American colonies of Spain and Portugal, stretching from the present-day western United States southward through Mexico, Central America and all of South America to Cape Horn, were now about 250 years old. The *conquistadores*, Spanish military leaders, came here soon after the earliest explorers. They included such daring and ruthless men as Hernando Cortez, who in 1519 conquered the empire of the Aztec Indians in Mexico, and Francisco Pizarro, who in 1532 defeated and subdued the empire of another highly civilized Indian nation, the Incas of Peru. Central and South America were rather sparsely inhabited by various Indian groups that differed greatly physically and culturally. Except for the Aztecs, the Incas and the Mayas in Yucatan and Guatemala, most of the South American Indians were barbarous and warlike.

The European conquerors used the Indians as forced labor to extract gold and silver from the rich mines of the New World. Later, Spanish and Portuguese settlers arrived in large numbers, but could not easily fill such a vast expanse of land. Black slaves from Africa were also introduced, although they were used chiefly in areas where agriculture rather than mining was the principal occupation. The whites and Indians in Latin America intermarried quite freely, and Spanish and Indian blood became mixed on a large scale. Thus a new culture grew up, one that was neither wholly Spanish nor wholly Indian.

The colonies were ruled largely for the benefit of the European homelands. Considering the fact that during the eighteenth century eighty-five per cent of the average annual production of gold in the whole world came from Latin America, it is not surprising that Spain and Portugal kept a tight rein on the colonies. Nevertheless, the frontier-type culture was passing, the general population and the cities in particular were growing, and the Enlightenment was felt in the far reaches of the two empires. As we have seen, both Spain and Portugal had enlightened despots as rulers and their policies benefited the colonies.

Trading restrictions were eased. The Catholic Church carried considerable weight both economically and culturally, but it was not as powerful as it once had been. The people were about one generation away from throwing off Spanish and Portuguese rule, but talk of independence and more than one small uprising indicated that the Latin

American colonies, too, were nearly ready to go their own way. The increase in the number of *mestizos*, the descendants of a mixture of Spanish or Portuguese with Indian blood, largely accounted for this growing urge to be rid of European rule. The *mestizos* felt no natural loyalty to the European world.

The Spanish colonies were organized into four extensive viceroyalties, the last of which was established in 1776. Within these areas were captaincy generals — much like states or provinces within a nation. A well-organized bureaucracy, with firm rules and regulations as to rank and duty, functioned surprisingly efficiently considering the great distances involved and the time it took to communicate within a viceroyalty, not to mention with the seat of government in far-off Madrid. It was no easy task to manage an empire so extensive, composed of all kinds of land from equatorial forests to lofty mountains, and inhabited in part by a conquered race — the various Indian tribes and nations.

New Spain was the largest of the viceroyalties. It included not only Mexico and all of Central America down to Panama, plus Cuba and other islands of the Caribbean, but also Florida and the whole expanse of territory west of the Mississippi River to the Pacific Ocean, except for what was later known as the Oregon Territory. Mexico City, with a population of a little more than 100,000, which made it larger than any of the cities of Europe except London, Paris and St. Petersburg, was the capital of New Spain. Mexico had a larger population than the thirteen British colonies, while the Spanish-American upper classes, long established in the New World, far outdid their counterparts in the North American colonies in elegance. The native Indian population was mistreated and repressed economically, but Mexico as a country prospered. The silver mines employed thousands in hard, dangerous work, and produced about half the world's output of silver. Textile and other manufacturing was conducted on a sizable scale.

Leading figures in the government of New Spain were José de Galvez (1720–87) and Antonio Maria Bucareli y Ursúa (1717–79). The former, after serving in New Spain from 1765 to 1772 in the high post of visitor general—a job which entailed inspecting the operations of the govern-ments of the various colonies—returned to Spain. Galvez became a major influence in the Council of the Indies, the body of government officials who watched over and set policy for Spain's colonial empire, and in 1775 he was named minister general. He labored to secure more liberal trade regulations for the colonies. Bucareli, who had served in the army, was captain general of Cuba when he was appointed viceroy of New Spain, a post he held for eight years. As an administrator he brought peace and prosperity and became a popular figure. He emphasized the settlement and building of defense positions along the Pacific Coast. One Spanish fort, in the bay at Acapulco in Mexico, was destroyed by an earthquake in 1776.

Although the Spaniards long laid claim to Texas, among other lands north of the Rio Grande, it was only in the mid-dle and late eighteenth century that they occupied Texas to any noticeable extent. They were almost constantly at war with the Indians over what later was the southwestern United States. Their difficulties with the Apaches and Comanches became worse after the Indians, in the late seventeenth century, learned to fight on horseback.

The viceroyalty of New Granada, established in 1717, lay south of New Spain. It included what later became the nations of Colombia, Ecuador, Panama and Venezuela, with Bogota as the capital. Manuel Antonio Flores was appointed viceroy in 1776. He soon ran into trouble with the home government because the overlords in Spain thought he was not energetic enough in collecting funds for the treasury.

Peru, which included Chile and until 1776 had included much more of South America, was the oldest viceroyalty and, in some ways, still the heart of Spanish America. About 250 years before, Francisco Pizarro and his small band of troops had conquered the Inca kingdom and laid the cornerstone of Spanish wealth and power in the Western Hemisphere. Pizarro founded Lima, an entirely new city, which now had a population of around 50,000, and at one time had been the capital of the whole Spanish overseas empire. Peru had two viceroys in 1776. Don Manuel Amat y Junient departed that year after five years in office. He was an able administrator who strengthened the royal authority and planned further development of Peru's resources. He was succeeded by Don Manuel Guirior.

The new viceroyalty was that of the Rio de la Plata, named for the estuary formed by the Parana and Uruguay rivers. It included present-day Argentina, Uruguay, Paraguay and part of Bolivia with Buenos Aires, then a town of about 20,000 population, as the capital. This southern region lagged behind the rest of Spanish America. It was important, however, in the defense of Spanish possessions against the Portuguese to the north and against the British who were showing interest in the area and whose seapower worried the Spaniards. Pedro de Cevallos was appointed the first viceroy and he sailed from Cadiz, Spain, in November, 1776, to take up his post.

The pampas, the grassy treeless plains found in Argentina, supported large herds of cattle, much as the western plains of the United States did later. The pampas also produced the gaucho—the equivalent of the American cowboy—who was a familiar figure from the early eighteenth century on. A horseman, and an individualist, the gaucho was also an Indian fighter who regularly battled the Indians of the pampas.

Brazil, which by itself occupies nearly half the continent, belonged to Portugal and went through much the same stages and changes as did the Spanish lands. Its growth and development were due more to the efforts of the colonists than to the home government. The seat of government was Rio de Janeiro, then a city of about 43,000. From 1769 to 1778, the viceroy was Luis d'Almeida Portugal, Marquis of Lavradio. Gold and diamond mining were important in Brazil and the chief mining center was the town of Ouro Préto in eastern Brazil, in the Minas Gerais district. Ouro Préto was a typical mining town in the eighteenth century, growing and brawling, and probably the liveliest city in Brazil at the time.

In spite of the rush to get rich by finding gold and diamonds, Ouro Préto became a cultural center, too, with its own writers and other intellectuals who became well known as the Minas literary group. It was also the home of an unusual sculptor and of a man who tried to start a revolution. The sculptor was Aleijadhinho (1730–1814). His real name was Antonio Francisco Lisboa and he was a mulatto. Either through disease or injury, his hands and feet were almost useless and so his mallet and chisel had to be tied to his hands to enable him to work. He is remembered for his church carvings, in a baroque style, which can be seen today in Ouro Préto in the church of São Francisco. In fact, the whole city, much reduced in population from the boom days, is now a national museum, preserving its eighteenth-century streets and buildings, including the oldest theater in South America.

The revolutionary was Tirandentes (1748–92), whose real name was José Joaquim da Silva Xavier. His nickname meant "tooth puller," and was bestowed on him because at one time he worked as a healer. Inspired by the American Revolution, Tirandentes led an unsuccessful revolution in the late 1780's and was executed.

Ever since the Spaniards had reached the area that eventually became the states of Texas, New Mexico, Arizona and California, they had been exploring, seeking gold, setting up missions and building forts. They now decided to go farther north than usual because of threatened encroachments on the Pacific Coast by the Russians and the British. Accordingly, Viceroy Bucareli dispatched Juan Bautista de Anza (1735–88) in 1775 on an expedition northward. Anza was one of the ablest of the Spanish frontiersmen and he pushed on to the site of the future city of San Francisco, which he reached in late June, 1776. His expedition stayed until fall, building a fort and dedicating a mission. They called the settlement Yerba Buena.

Meanwhile, back in Philadelphia—

9

Philadelphia

July 4, 1776

And so, on July 4, 1776, while people of all lands, races and religions around the world were:

governing nations
criticizing the way nations were governed
composing music
exploring unknown parts of the world
painting pictures
trading with distant lands for exotic goods and Black slaves
writing books
manufacturing goods of all kinds
conducting scientific experiments
and living the ordinary life of ordinary people,

the delegates to the Second Continental Congress were assembled in Philadelphia to complete the formal steps necessary to proclaim their defiance of Great Britain and

King George III, and their irrevocable determination to launch an independent nation.

Independence had, in fact, been voted two days earlier, and some of those present expected July 2 to be the date of any future observances. But while a resolution for independence had been approved, the delegates wished to adopt a more formal statement. Thus the vote on July 4, unanimous except that the New York delegation still awaited instructions from home, officially approved the Declaration of Independence, drafted by Thomas Jefferson.

John Dunlap, a Philadelphia printer, worked that night to have copies of the Declaration ready the next day. Taking time to arrange a proper celebration, those in charge first had it read publicly in Philadelphia on July 8. A copy reached General Washington in New York the next day, and he had his troops assembled to hear it read to them. It was July 18 before the Declaration was officially proclaimed in Boston. Meanwhile, a copy engrossed on parchment was being prepared, but it was August 2 before it was ready to be signed by the delegates to the Congress. American independence was now a fact, providing those who favored it could defeat the British Empire in armed conflict.

The philosophy behind the Declaration came across the ocean from Europe, out of the Enlightenment of France and the earlier political philosophers of England. It was in that spirit that Jefferson used such phrases as:

> Laws of Nature and of Nature's God
> all men are created equal
> certain unalienable rights
> life, liberty and the pursuit of happiness
> the consent of the governed

The war the document brought on was, in the end, only one of the results of the Declaration. Despots, no matter how enlightened they might be, could not help but hope these flaming words would not be taken seriously and literally by their own subjects. The colonists' words and actions were unquestionably an inspiration to those who brought about the French Revolution of 1789. Everywhere, at least in liberal and Enlightenment circles, it was freely predicted that this was the dawn of a new age for the world. America seemed to have proved that the ideas of the Age of Reason could be put to practical use. The myth of America as somehow different from the rest of the world got its start. Here great new things would happen.

Millions of people around the world in 1776 who might have been most interested in what the Declaration said, and in what it could conceivably mean to them, never heard of it. The descendants of these people — Asian peasants and African Blacks, for example — did learn about it several generations later, in the twentieth century. And when they did, they too demanded "life, liberty and the pursuit of happiness," although it is difficult, if not impossible, to prove how much influence the Declaration of Independence of 1776 had on the independence movements in Asian and African colonies after World War II. In any event, the rebels of the eighteenth and the twentieth centuries, although separated by nearly 200 years in time, sought the same goal: the right, for better or for worse, to determine their own destinies, free of a distant and seemingly hostile rule.

Reading List

In the following list the publisher and the date of publication are those of the latest edition. Some of these books are available in paper as well as hardbound editions.

ANDERSON, M. S. *Eighteenth-Century Europe, 1713–1789.* New York: Oxford University Press, Inc., 1966.

ASHTON, T. S. *The Industrial Revolution, 1760–1830.* New York: Oxford University Press, Inc., 1948.

BERNARD, PAUL P. *Joseph II.* New York: Twayne Publishers, Inc., 1968.

BERTRAND, LOUIS, and PETRIE, SIR CHARLES. *The History of Spain.* 2nd ed. New York: Collier Books, 1971.

BRAILSFORD, H. N. *Voltaire.* New York: Oxford University Press, Inc., 1935.

CLARK, MANNING. *A Short History of Australia.* New York: New American Library, 1963.

CORBETT, JAMES A. *The Papacy: A Brief History.* Princeton: D. Van Nostrand Co., Inc., 1956.

CRANKSHAW, EDWARD. *Maria Theresa.* New York: The Viking Press, 1969.

CURTIS, EDMUND. *A History of Ireland.* 6th ed. New York: Barnes & Noble, Inc., 1950.

DAVIDSON, BASIL. *The African Slave Trade; Precolonial History, 1450–1850.* Boston: Little, Brown and Co., 1961.

DAVISON, RODERIC H. *Turkey.* Englewood Cliffs: Prentice-Hall, Inc., 1968.

FAGE, J. D. (ed.). *Africa Discovers Her Past.* New York: Oxford University Press, Inc., 1970.

FITZGERALD, C. P. *A Concise History of East Asia.* New York: Praeger Publishers, 1966.

FORSTER, ROBERT and FORSTER, ELBORG (eds.). *European Society in the Eighteenth Century.* New York: Harper & Row, Publishers, 1969.

GAGLIARDO, JOHN G. *Enlightened Despotism.* New York: Thomas Y. Crowell Co., 1967.

GAY, PETER. *The Enlightenment: An Interpretation; The Rise of Modern Paganism.* New York: Alfred A. Knopf, Inc., 1966.

GOODRICH, L. CARRINGTON. *A Short History of the Chinese People.* 3rd ed. New York: Harper & Row, Publishers, 1959.

HALECKI, O. *A History of Poland.* New York: Roy Publishers, 1966.

HEARDER, H. and WALEY, D. P. (eds.). *A Short History of Italy, from Classical Times to the Present Day.* New York: Cambridge University Press, 1963.

HITTI, PHILIP K. *The Arabs: A Short History.* 5th ed. New York: St. Martin's Press, 1968.

HOLT, P. M. *Egypt and the Fertile Crescent, 1516–1922: A Political History.* Ithaca: Cornell University Press, 1966.

HSU, IMMANUEL C. Y. *The Rise of Modern China.* New York: Oxford University Press, Inc., 1970.

HUGHES, PHILIP. *A Popular History of the Catholic Church.* New York: The Macmillan Co., 1947.

JONES, A. H. M. and MONROE, ELIZABETH. *A History of Ethiopia.* New York: Oxford University Press, Inc., 1935.

KENNEDY, MALCOLM D. *A Short History of Japan.* New York: New American Library, 1964.

LINDSAY, DONALD and WASHINGTON, E. S. *A Portrait of Britain from Peril to Pre-Eminence, 1688–1851*. New York: Oxford University Press, Inc., 1954.

LLOYD, ALAN. *The King Who Lost America: A Portrait of the Life and Times of George III*. Garden City: Doubleday & Co., Inc., 1971.

LOUGH, JOHN. *An Introduction to Eighteenth Century France*. New York: David McKay Co., Inc., 1970.

MCNAUGHT, KENNETH. *The Pelican History of Canada*. Baltimore: Penguin Books, 1969.

MCNEILL, WILLIAM H. *A World History*. 2nd ed. New York: Oxford University Press, Inc., 1971.

MALONE, DUMAS. *The Story of the Declaration of Independence*. New York: Oxford University Press, Inc., 1954.

OAKLEY, STEWART. *A Short History of Sweden*. New York: Frederick A. Praeger, Publishers, 1966.

OLIVA, L. JAY (ed.). *Catherine the Great*. Englewood Cliffs: Prentice-Hall, Inc., 1971.

OLIVER, ROLAND (ed.). *The Middle Age of African History*. New York: Oxford University Press, Inc., 1967.

OLIVER, ROLAND and FAGE, J. D. *A Short History of Africa*. 3rd ed. Baltimore: Penguin Books, 1970.

PADOVER, SAUL K. *The Life and Death of Louis XVI*. New York: Taplinger Publishing Co., 1963.

PALMER, R. R. *The Age of the Democratic Revolution; A Political History of Europe and America, 1760–1800*. Vol. I: The Challenge. Princeton: Princeton University Press, 1959.

PARET, PETER (ed.). *Frederick the Great: A Profile*. New York: Hill and Wang, 1972.

PETERSON, MERRILL D. *Thomas Jefferson and the New Nation*. New York: Oxford University Press, Inc., 1970.

RAEFF, MARC (ed.). *Catherine the Great: A Profile*. New York: Hill and Wang, 1972.

RIASANOVSKY, NICHOLAS V. *A History of Russia*. 2nd ed. New York: Oxford University Press, Inc., 1969.

ROBERTS, P. E. *History of British India, Under the Company and the Crown*. 3rd ed. Completed by T. G. P. Spear. New York: Oxford University Press, Inc., 1952.

RUDÉ, GEORGE (ed.). *The Eighteenth Century*. New York: The Free Press, 1965.

SIMON, W. M. *Germany: A Brief History*. New York: Random House, 1967.

SMITH, PRESERVED. *The Enlightenment, 1687–1776*. Vol. II (A History of Modern Culture). New York: Holt, Rinehart and Winston, Inc., 1934.

SNYDER, LOUIS L. (ed.). *Frederick the Great*. Englewood Cliffs: Prentice-Hall, Inc., 1971.

WATSON, J. STEVEN. *The Reign of George III, 1760–1815*. New York: Oxford University Press, Inc., 1960.

WILBER, DONALD N. *Iran: Past and Present*. Princeton: Princeton University Press, 1967.

WOODHOUSE, C. M. *A Short History of Modern Greece*. New York: Frederick A. Praeger, Publishers, 1968.

WORCESTER, DONALD E. and SCHAEFFER, WENDELL G. *The Growth and Culture of Latin America*. Vol. I: From Conquest to Independence. 2nd ed. New York: Oxford University Press, Inc., 1970.

Index